Compositioni varie per musica di camera
Opus 13

Recent Researches in Music

A-R Editions publishes seven series of critical editions, spanning the history of Western music, American music, and oral traditions.

Recent Researches in the Music of the Middle Ages and Early Renaissance
Charles M. Atkinson, general editor

Recent Researches in the Music of the Renaissance
James Haar, general editor

Recent Researches in the Music of the Baroque Era
Steven Saunders, general editor

Recent Researches in the Music of the Classical Era
Neal Zaslaw, general editor

Recent Researches in the Music of the Nineteenth and Early Twentieth Centuries
Rufus Hallmark, general editor

Recent Researches in American Music
John M. Graziano, general editor

Recent Researches in the Oral Traditions of Music
Philip V. Bohlman, general editor

Each edition in *Recent Researches* is devoted to works by a single composer or to a single genre. The content is chosen for its high quality and historical importance and is edited according to the scholarly standards that govern the making of all reliable editions.

For information on establishing a standing order to any of our series, or for editorial guidelines on submitting proposals, please contact:

A-R Editions, Inc.
Middleton, Wisconsin

800 736-0070 (North American book orders)
608 836-9000 (phone)
608 831-8200 (fax)
http://www.areditions.com

RECENT RESEARCHES IN THE MUSIC OF THE BAROQUE ERA, 169

Biagio Marini

Compositioni varie per musica di camera Opus 13

Edited by Thomas D. Dunn

A-R Editions, Inc.
Middleton, Wisconsin

Performance parts are available from the publisher.

A-R Editions, Inc., Middleton, Wisconsin
© 2011 by A-R Editions, Inc.

All rights reserved. No part of this book may be reproduced or transmitted in any form by any electronic or mechanical means (including photocopying, recording, or information storage and retrieval) without permission in writing from the publisher.

The purchase of this edition does not convey the right to perform it in public, nor to make a recording of it for any purpose. Such permission must be obtained in advance from the publisher.

A-R Editions is pleased to support scholars and performers in their use of *Recent Researches* material for study or performance. Subscribers to any of the *Recent Researches* series, as well as patrons of subscribing institutions, are invited to apply for information about our "Copyright Sharing Policy."

Printed in the United States of America

ISBN-13: 978-0-89579-690-5
ISBN-10: 0-89579-690-2
ISSN: 0484-0828

∞ The paper used in this publication meets the minimum requirements of the American National Standard for Information Sciences—Permanence of Paper for Printed Library Materials, ANSI Z39.48-1992.

Contents

Acknowledgments vi

Introduction vii
   Marini in the 1630s vii
   The *Compositioni varie* vii
   Texts, Translations, and Commentaries viii
   Notes xvii

Plates xix

Compositioni varie per musica di camera, Opus 13
   (Numbers 6–18 are with violins)
   Dedication 2
     1. Torna l'inverno, frigido *(CC or TT)* 3
     2. Ecco ch'io manco *(AT)* 10
     3. Miratemi o begl'occhi *(AA or CC)* 15
     4. Deh, come in un momento *(ATB)* 21
     5. Qui, dove il sol *(ATB)* 28
     6. Pastorella *(CB)* 37
     7. Non fuggir, vago augello *(AT)* 47
     8. Che non senta per voi *(AB)* 54
     9. Or che Giovanni *(CTB)* 60
     10. Già brutto non son io *(TTB)* 67
     11. Or so come da sè *(ATB)* 76
     12. Su l'ali del tempo *(ATB)* 84
     13. Spars'ho in pianto *(TTB or TT)* 93
     14. Aure placide e volanti *(CTB)* 103
     15. Per torbido mare *(ATB)* 111
     16. Io, che piansi *(CCB, CTB, or TTB)* 117
     17. Una fanciulla *(CTB)* 126
     18. Addio begl'occhi *(CCATB)* 131

Critical Report 145
   Source 145
   Editorial Procedures 145
   Critical Notes 146
   Notes 149

Acknowledgments

Years ago the late Professor Claude Palisca urged me to investigate Biagio Marini's vocal music as a pendant to my study of that composer's works for instruments, and this edition represents an outgrowth of that ongoing study. As other scholars working in this area have indicated plans to publish editions of some of Marini's other collections of vocal music, I settled on his perhaps less well-known opus 13. This work was particularly challenging due to the need to reconstruct violin parts for many of the pieces as well as missing vocal parts for the final piece.

Once again Dr. Martin P. Morell proved himself an invaluable source of advice and suggestions concerning translations of the sometimes difficult texts. To paraphrase a line in Marini's dedication of the *Compositioni varie* to Abbot Scaglia, some of the phrases in the translation are more Dr. Morell's than mine. Many thanks are due to Anna Hołyk of the Biblioteka Uniwersytecka at the University of Wrocław for permission to publish transcriptions based on their unique copy of the print and for allowing us to include facsimile images from the collection. Professor Wayne Hobbs most kindly sent me scanned images of those pages in Anerio's *Teatro armonico spirituale* (Rome, 1619) containing that composer's setting of the "Or che Giovanni" text. The Repertorio della Poesia Italiana in Musica, 1500–1700, an internet database edited by Angelo Pompilio of the University of Bologna, Department of Music and Theater, was helpful in tracking down the authors of a few of the texts. Finally, the editorial staff of A-R Editions is once again due thanks for their patient and meticulous work during the editing and final production stages.

Introduction

Marini in the 1630s

In a letter addressed to an unnamed "Serenissimo et Clementissimo Signore" dated 15 December 1628, Biagio Marini indicated that he was requesting a leave of absence from his position as *maestro di capella* to the Wittelsbach court at Neuburg an der Donau, claiming that "l'aria di questo paese non mi conferischi più" (the atmosphere of this place no longer benefits me).[1] Whether "l'aria" was simply weather—harsh winters perhaps—or was related to other issues, personal and/or political, can only be conjectured.[2] Documents dated 1627 in Marini's home city of Brescia affirm that he still held property and citizen status there.[3] He had also established connections in Milan and Bergamo. A document in the archives of the Milan *Duomo*, dated 10 February 1631, notes a request from him to be considered for a position in that institution.[4] The request was apparently "tabled," but he may have held another position in the city between September 1631 and November 1632.[5] He performed in Bergamo in April of 1632.[6] In 1635 his *Madrigaletti*, opus 9, was finally published—it had been dedicated 1 July 1625. Although no copies of his opp. 10–12 have survived it is not unreasonable to assume that they also appeared during the 1630s. His third and final marriage must have occurred around 1635, judging from the approximate ages of three children from that union as given in later documents. This betrothal was to a Margarita Taeggia who had Milanese connections and may have been a member of the Rognoni family.[7] The fates of the two children from his first marriage, Julia and Manfredo, who accompanied him to Neuburg in 1623, are unknown, as is that of his second wife, Helena Hanin. In a *polizze d'estimo,* filed by Marini in Brescia on 23 July 1641, the latter is simply—and erroneously—described as his "prima molie" [*sic*], with no mention whether or not she was deceased. If her second child by Marini, Giovanni Nicola, was born around 1629, his birth may have taken place in Italy rather than Neuburg.[8]

Yet in his *Compositioni varie*, opus 13, and the *Corona melodica*, opus 15, dated 1641 and 1644, respectively, he was still calling himself a cavalier "del Sereniss. Palatino di Noiburg." The date of his actual return to the service of the Wittelsbach court is uncertain, but it most likely took place in early 1644.[9]

The *Compositioni varie*

The *Compositioni varie per musica di camera a due, tre, quattro, cinque, voci, e parte con due violini*, opus 13, is the only surviving collection of secular vocal music by Marini between the *Madrigaletti* and the *Concerto terzo delle musica da camera*, the latter published as opus 16 in Milan in 1649. As with the 1641 *polizze* mentioned above, the dedication of opus 13 indicates that Marini was maintaining a presence in Brescia, including connections with religious and monastic institutions. The dedicatee, Valeriano Scaglia (d. 1656), was *abbate generale* of the Olivetian monastery in Brescia during 1639–42.[10] It is not impossible that he could have been the author of some of the texts, which might explain Marini's assertion that the pieces are being presented "to him as his own" (see page 2 for the dedication text and its translation).

The collection comprises eighteen works (see table 1). The phrase "per musica di camera" in the title is appropriate. With the exception of the final work, all the pieces are either duets or trios, with parts for two violins indicated for all but the first five pieces. The title is misleading as there are no pieces for four singing voices. Both violin partbooks were destroyed when the university library in Breslau (now Wrocław) was bombed at the end of the Second World War (see the editorial procedures of the critical report for a discussion of the reconstructions of these parts in the present edition). Thus the collection may be said to counterbalance an earlier collection by Marini in which the phrase "per le musiche di camera" also appears in the title: the *Concerti a quatro 5. 6. voci, & instromenti*, opus 7, which had been planned and possibly assembled around 1624 but not published until ten years later.

The adjective *varie* in the title is appropriate as well; the eighteen works in the print range over a variety of musical forms and styles. In some, the melodic and rhythmic vocabulary suggests the term "dance song," continuing a tradition that had already flourished twenty years earlier in collections such as Sigismondo d'India's *Le musiche e balli a quattro voci* and Marini's own *Scherzi e canzonette*, opus 5.[11] Three pieces in opus 13 come closest to such a designation: the trios "Aure placide e volanti," "Per torbido mare," and "Su l'ali del tempo," although a case could also be made for the "Pastorella" duet.

TABLE 1
Biagio Marini, *Compositioni varie*, Opus 13

Title	Scoring	*Finalis*
1. Torna l'inverno, frigido	CC (or TT), B.c.	A
2. Ecco ch'io manco	AT, B.c.	D
3. Miratemi o begl'occhi	AA (or CC), B.c.	D
4. Deh, come in un momento	ATB, B.c.	D
5. Qui, dove il sol	ATB, B.c.	D
6. Pastorella	CB, Vn. 1-2, B.c.	F
7. Non fuggir, vago augello	AT, Vn. 1-2, B.c.	D
8. Che non senta per voi	AB, Vn. 1-2, B.c.	D
9. Or che Giovanni	CTB, Vn. 1-2, B.c.	D
10. Già brutto non son io	TTB, Vn. 1-2, B.c.	G
11. Or so come da sè	ATB, Vn. 1-2, B.c.	C
12. Su l'ali del tempo	ATB, Vn. 1-2, B.c.	C
13. Spars'ho in pianto	TTB (or TT), Vn. 1-2, B.c.	C
14. Aure placide e volanti	CTB, Vn. 1-2, B.c.	D
15. Per torbido mare	ATB, Vn. 1-2, B.c.	G
16. Io, che piansi	CCB (or CTB, or TTB), Vn. 1-2, B.c.	D
17. Una fanciulla	CTB, Vn. 1-2, B.c.	D
18. Addio begl'occhi	CCATB, Vn. 1-2, B.c.	D

Although many of the works are strophic, they do not necessarily repeat the same music for each strophe. "Già brutto non son io" and "Or so come da sè" are good examples; the music for the various strophes is similar but not exactly identical. By contrast, "Torna l'inverno, frigido" and "Qui, dove il sol" are through-composed even though the texts are strophic. About half of the pieces have ritornelli, two of which are labeled *a beneplacito*. Both "Spars'ho in pianto" and "Io, che piansi" could be regarded as early examples of the cantata, as they contain sections variously *in stile recitativo*, *aria*, or *mezz'aria*. Finally, "Or che Giovanni" could be classified as a short oratorio.

Unlike Marini's opus 7, there does not appear to be a common thread running through the texts, although many share common situations: an amenable arcadian refuge, withholding of sexual favors, or flight from a would-be suitor. The accuracy of the texts as printed by Vincenti is variable. Wording and spelling can vary between partbooks, and in some pieces, such as "Già brutto non son io" and "Per torbido mare," the meaning of entire lines and phrases is obscure or virtually incomprehensible, perhaps the result of the omission of a key word or a radical misspelling. Welding of music and text is also made with varying degrees of success. Scansion is at times carefully followed but in other instances it is difficult to avoid the the impression that Marini was recycling stock musical gestures, some conceived independently of any specific text.

Only two pieces—"Pastorella" and "Per torbido mare"—have a B-flat signature indicating *cantus mollis*. Eleven—more than half—have D as *finalis*. Some, such as "Miratemi o begl'occhi," "Deh, come in un momento," and "Or so come da sè," span a wide tonal range, whereas the dance songs—"Su l'ali del tempo" and "Aure placide," for instance—are more restrictive in terms of cadences.

Texts, Translations, and Commentaries

1. *Torna l'inverno, frigido*

Torna l'inverno, frigido
Co 'l suo fiero rigor,
E con l'aspetto rigido
Scaccia l'estivo ardor;
Ma non tempra l'arsura
Che d'ogni tempo nel mio petto dura.

Gli arboscelli si spogliano
Del frondoso vestir,
Par ch'i prati si dogliano
Che più non puon fiorir;
Ma nell'arso mio core
Sempre più cresce e si rinforza amore.

Le nevi i monti altissimi
Già fanno biancheggiar
E da giacci durissimi
Coperto il tutto par;
Ma l'amoroso foco
Spegner non puote in me ne tempo o loco.

A venti che gareggiano
Co 'l caldo sospirar,
A piogge che pareggiano
Il lungo lagrimar,
Veggio che vien l'inverno,
Ma questo passa e il mio resta eterno.

* * *

Frigid winter returns
with its fierce inclemency
and with stern appearance
drives away summer's heat;
but it does not temper the fire
that remains in my breast for all seasons.

The tree branches divest themselves
of their leafy vestment,
and the meadows appear to grieve
because they can no longer bloom;
but love continually grows and gains strength
in my consumed heart.

The highest mountains are already
made white with snow
and everything appears covered
with the hardest ice;
but neither time nor place
can extinguish the amorous fire within me.

By the winds that contend
with [my] warm sighing,
by the rains that resemble
drawn-out weeping,
I see that winter draws nigh,
But it passes, whereas mine remains eternal.

Commentary. The text comprises four six-line strophes with rhyme scheme *ababcc*, a shortened version of the *ottava rima*, so to speak. The subject is familiar: a pastoral landscape contrasted with the speaker's emotional turmoil.[12] But this time there is a twist: now the pastoral landscape is bare and frigid in contrast with the *ardore* of the speaker's condition, the latter described in lines 5 and 6 of each strophe. Marini sets each of these concluding pairs as a refrain, thus fashioning a rondo-like structure.[13] The initial measures are in a melodic/rhythmic style suggesting a *balletto* and move quickly across a sequence of minor chords from the initial A minor through G minor to D minor. The close proximity of C to C♯, F to F♯, and B to B♭ intensifies the unsettled mood. By contrast, the refrain is in a quasi-recitative style and clearly inhabits the *durus* region with chords on A, E, and even B. None of the subsequent strophes have the same music, although the third is the same length as the first.

This is the first of three pieces (the others are nos. 3 and 16) in the *Compositioni varie* in which performance in alternate vocal ranges is indicated, in this case by two tenors. The actual downward interval of transposition is not specified, but it is presumably by an octave.

2. Ecco ch'io manco

Ecco ch'io manco, o Dori,
Dori spietata, o Dio,
Ecco ch'io moro;
E a miei cocenti ardori
Non dai pur, infedel,
Qualche ristoro.
Perfida, e così stimai il viver mio!
Addio beltà crudel,
Io moro, addio.

* * *

Behold, I'm swooning, O Dori,
pitiless Dori, O God!
Behold, I'm dying;
and yet to my seething passion,
faithless one,
you give no respite.

Traitress! Thus you value my life!
Farewell, cruel beauty,
I die, farewell.

Commentary. The brevity of "Ecco ch'io manco" counters the expansiveness of "Torna l'inverno." With its alternating lengths of five, six, and seven syllables (three in the final line) the text is definitely in the style of Chiabrera and could be termed a *scherzo* or *canzonetta*.[14] Its quick, fade-out ending recalls Monteverdi's "Sì ch'io vorrei morire," although here sexual fulfillment is apparently denied. The opening lines are set to a harmonic progression somewhat akin to the romanesca, and the piece is spiced with 7-6 and 7-5 suspensions and teasing phrygian cadences.

The title in the partbooks contains the phrase "All'Illustrissimo Sig. Nicoletto Donato."

3. Miratemi o begl'occhi

Miratemi o begl'occhi, o crudo o pio
Sia 'l guardo, egual diletto Amor ne prende;
Se mi toglie la vita un fier desio
Una vista gentil poi me la rende.

Miratemi o begl'occhi, o qual sent'io
Gioia per voi che all'anima s'apprende,
Si spazia fuor di sè lo spirto mio
Quando 'l bel vostro lume al cor mi scende.

Miratemi o begl'occhi, un dolce giro
Se rivolgete in me, mi sollevate
Dal cieco abisso al luminoso empiro.

Miratemi o begl'occhi, o luci amate,
Miratemi, e di lei per cui sospiro
Tempri la crudeltà vostra pietate.

* * *

Look upon me, O lovely eyes. Be ye cruel
or kindly, love takes equal delight.
If a fierce desire deprives me of life
a fair vision then restores it.

Look upon me, O lovely eyes. Oh how I feel
joy through you who cleave to the soul.
My spirit soars, beside itself
when your beauteous light descends into my heart.

Look upon me, O lovely eyes. If you turn
a sweet passing glance towards me, you raise me
from the bottomless abyss into the luminous realm.

Look upon me, O lovely eyes, O beloved orbs,
Look upon me, and on account of her for whom I sigh
may your pity restrain her cruelty.

Commentary. This rather knotty sonnet by Gian Francesco Maia Materdona was published in his *Della rime, parte prima* (Venice, 1629).[15] It may be a trope or comment on Pietro Petracci's "Perché non mi mirate, occhi crudi o pietosi," which was published in 1615 and set by d'India in his *Il terzo libro dei madrigali a cinque voci*.[16] In both texts the eyes can be either cruel or full of pity, but in the final lines of Marini's text it is unclear if the eyes belong to the beloved or someone else.

The music spans both the *durus* and *mollis* tonal areas, the harmonic fabric ranging from chords on E major (m. 6, for instance) to G-minor sonorities. Short sections in triple meter serve to provide contrasting settings of the opening phrase "Miratemi o begl'occhi" when it is repeated in lines 5 and 12. The descending figure on that phrase of text in measures 4–12 may have been a stock one for the composer; he used it in the trio "Bella cantatrice" in his opus 3 from 1620. Text painting is generously applied, most strikingly at "mi sollevate / Dal cieco abisso al luminoso empiro" in measures 59–68, where the first alto (or canto) must span the range of an octave and a sixth.

The canto partbook indicates that alternate performance by two *soprani* should be performed "a la quinta alta," while the basso continuo partbook has the phrase "Alti o Canti sonando alla quarta bassa." The last four words, however, most likely refer to the actual continuo line and not the singers' music.

4. Deh, come in un momento

Deh, come in un momento,
Qual ombra, o strale, o vento,
Veggio da questo petto
Sparito ogni diletto;
Come si tosto giunge
Il dolor che mi punge
Su l'intimo del core,
E chi da gl'occhi fore
Mi trae di pianto un mare,
E d'aspre pene amare
M'ingombra l'alma e 'l seno.
Ah voi, ch'in un baleno,
Turbati di disdegno,
Occhi mi date segno
Che v'annoi mia vita,
E che da voi sparita
Sia questa luce ond'io
Ardo di bel desio.
Non date al mio fallire
Cotanto di martire.
Pietate, ohimè,[a] pietate,
Non possa[b] feritate
Nel vostro bel sereno;
Ma voi, beati a pieno
Con vostr'almi splendori,
Beate gl'altrui cori.

* * *

Ah, how suddenly, as a fleeting shade,
arrow, or gust of wind,
I see that from this breast
every pleasure has vanished;
how often the sadness
that pierces me reaches
the depths of my heart,
and which draws out
a sea of tears from my eyes,
and weighs down my soul and bosom
with harsh, bitter pain.
Ah, as in a flash of lightning,
ye eyes, troubled by disdain,
give me a sign
that my life is wearisome to you,
and that the light in which
I burn from pleasant desire
is gone from you.
Do not reward my shortcomings
with so much suffering.
Have pity, alas, have pity,
for there can be no wounding
while in your serene bosom;
but may you, fully blessed
with your noble splendors,
bless other hearts as well.

Note. The words are (a) "occhi" in Rasi's original text; and (b) "possi" in Marini's version, for which I follow Rasi.

Commentary. The text is by Francesco Rasi, whose own setting, for solo voice, appeared a third of a century earlier in his *Vaghezze di musica*.[17] The declamatory opening provides one of the more arresting moments in the *Compositioni*, evincing a direct response to the text rather than a grafting on of recycled musical gestures. The sudden B-flat major at line 3 (m. 7) followed by the drooping 6-5 suspensions illustrating the departure of "every pleasure" adds to the initial instability of the piece. The music subsequently indulges in a variety of styles. At the line "E chi da gl'occhi fore" (mm. 21–24) the continuo begins an ostinato on the descending tetrachord, A–G–F–E, its sevenfold iterations illustrating the "sea of tears" and "harsh, bitter pain."[18] By contrast, the following section, beginning at the line "Ah voi, ch'in un baleno" (m. 50), is more *in stile recitativo*. Triple meter and another falling bass line return, in a *mollis* tonal area, at "Ardo di bel desio," while the subsequent "Non date al mio fallire" moves into the sharp area with chords on E major. The final line, "Beate gl'altrui cori," is treated in a similar manner to "Ardo" with close points of imitation.

5. Qui, dove il sol

Qui, dove il sol con temperato lume
Serena il cielo in un co 'l ciel le menti,
E i pastorelli i lor canori accenti
Destar di poggio in poggio han per costume,

Qui, dove il monte ombreggia ondeggia il fiume,
Rinfrescan l'ombra increspan l'aure i venti,
Sondon[a] l'herbette i mansueti armenti,
Spiegan gli augei le lascivette piume,

Qui, dove i puri e trasparenti umori
Fanno specchio a le fronde e 'l bel terreno,
Tutto spira delizie e tutto amori,

Qui vieni, o Cintia,[b] in questo sito ameno;
Corremo io dolci frutti e tu bei fiori,
Tu nel bel prato ed io nel tuo bel seno.

* * *

Here where the sun with moderate light
illuminates the sky and with it the spirit,

and the shepherds, as is their wont, raise
their melodious accents from hill to hill,

Here where the mountain storm rouses the stream,
the breezes refresh the shade,
the meek flocks browse the short grass,
the birds unfold their wanton feathers,

Here where the pure, clear waters
mirror the leafy terrain,
everything breathes sweetness and and love,

Come, O Cynthia, to this pleasant spot.
Let us gather (things), I sweet fruits and you pretty flowers,
You in the lovely meadow and I on your beautiful bosom.

Note. In Gino Rizzo's edition of the text, the words are (a) "Tondon" and (b) "Mirzia."

Commentary. The text is from Materdona's *Della rime, parte prima*.[19] A "Cynthia" had been addressed or invoked a number of times in Marini's opus 7. This is her only reference in opus 13, however, her name being changed from "Mirzia" in Materdona's original text. Here, as in "Non fuggir, vago augello," the pastoral landscape is inviting, rather than bleak as in "Torna l'inverno," and serves as a venue for escape. Entirely through-composed, the music fashioned for this sonnet is at times leisurely and expansive, most notably for the last three lines, which are drawn out by extended use of imitation and sequence. Contrast is provided by the brisk triple-meter sections, the first one notable for its engaging use of hemiola.

6. Pastorella

Pastorella
Vaga e bella,
Non partire,
Non fuggire,
Che se fuggi
Tu mi struggi.

Torna, torna
Faccia adorna,
Porgi aita,
Che la vita
Di te priva
Non e viva.

Ma, crudele,
Le querele
Sdegni intanto;
Del mio pianto
Non rispondi,
Pur t'ascondi.

Ecco almeno
T'apro il seno
O mio amore.
Svella il core
S'hai pur gioia
Ch'io mi moia;

Che godrai
Che vedrai
Da la salma
Partir l'alma
Per servirti,
Per gradirti.

* * *

O shepherdess,
fair and beautiful,
do not leave,
do not flee,
for if you fly from me
you destroy me.

Turn, turn
pretty countenance,
bring solace,
for life
without you
is lifeless.

But, cruel one,
my complaints
you still disdain;
to my lamentation
you do not reply,
rather you hide.

Lo then, at least
I open my breast to you,
oh my love.
Pluck out my heart
if you take joy
in my dying;

For then you shall
enjoy seeing
the spirit depart
from the flesh
to serve you,
to please you.

Commentary. Although the soprano-bass scoring of these five stanzas at first suggests a *dialogo* between a shepherdess and her suitor, the speaker heard throughout the text seems to be solely the latter. A comparison may be drawn with Chiabrera's "Clori amorosa," set by Monteverdi in his *Scherzi musicali* of 1607. Like Marini's work, it comprises five stanzas, this time consisting of nine *quinario* lines, and may be heard as the voice of an individual speaker beseeching a shepherdess for sexual favors. The stock phrase "porgi aita" followed by the rhyming "vita" at the end of the subsequent line occurs in both texts, as does the prediction "vedrai" in the respective final stanzas.

This is the only piece in the collection with F as *finalis*. All sections cadence on this pitch and the piece keeps to the flat area throughout, with A-flats appearing at "Tu mi struggi." Both the corrente-like ritornelli and the alternation of voices suggest that initial performances of the work may have involved choreography.[20]

7. Non fuggir, vago augello

Non fuggir, vago augello, affrena il volo,
Che non tendo a tuoi danni o visco o rete;

Che s'a me libertà cerco e quiete,
Porte non deggio in servitute e'n duolo.

Ben io fuggo a ragion nemico stuolo
Di gravi cure in quest'ombre secrete,
Ove sol per goder, sicure e liete,
Poch'ore teco, alla città m'involo.

Qui più sereno è il ciel, più l'aria pura,
Più dolci l'acque, e più cortese e bella
L'alte richezze sue scopre natura.

O mente umana, al proprio ben rubella!
Vede tanta sua pace e non la cura,
E stima porto ov' ha flutto e procella.

* * *

Do not flee, pretty bird, stay your flight,
lest I set a snare or net at your peril;
for I seek freedom and peace for myself
and should not place you in servitude and sorrow.

Well I flee, because of the evil throng
of heavy cares, to these secret shades
to enjoy alone a few secure, happy
hours with you, before I hasten back to the city.

Here the sky is more serene, the air purer,
the water sweeter, and nature reveals her lofty
riches to be more pleasing and beautiful.

O human thought, a thief unto itself!
So much it sees its peace and not its cares,
and regards flood and storm a safe haven.

Commentary. The sonnet is by Celio Magno and was published in his *Rime* (1600).[21] As with "Qui, dove il sol" it expresses delight in a pastoral refuge offering escape from stress and care. The music is through-composed and proceeds without any major halts for sectional articulation. The line "O mente humana, al proprio ben rubella!" is stressed by the use of longer note values and a three-fold repetition in A minor, D minor, and G major, respectively, providing still another example of Marini's preoccupation with harmonic movement by fifths. Although parts for two violins were included in the source there are no true ritornelli indicated. Presumably the instruments played during the brief periods when the singers were silent. The reconstructions are based on the initial melodic idea in the singers' parts.

8. Che non senta per voi

Che non senta per voi tormenti e guai,
Ch'il cor non mi consumi aspro veleno,
Ch'io non adori i vostri dolci rai,
Ch'io non sia di desir e d'amor pieno,
Che in queste braccia Amor vi stringa mai,
Che mai v'abbia a goder dentro al mio seno,
Quest'e proprio un cercar quand'arde 'l cielo
Su l'arene del mar le brine e 'l gelo.

* * *

That I not feel torments and woes for you,
that bitter venom not consume my heart,
that I not adore your gentle rays,
that I not be full of love and desire,
that in these arms love never holds you,
that you never find enjoyment within my breast,
this indeed is to be sought when the sky burns
and yet there is rime and ice on the seashore.

Commentary. The sense of this *ottava rima* text suggests a division into six lines plus two: the first six begin with "Che" and the last two offer a resolution. Yet Marini's placement of the ritornello between lines 4 and 5 indicates he may have had two four-line verses in mind.[22] The alternation of triple meter and common time has elements of a palindrome, with lines 3 ("Ch'io non adori . . .") and 5 ("Che in queste braccia . . .") set to the same meter and music. The sprightly, uncomplicated music emphasizes the frivolous side of the text. The reconstructed violin parts are based on the melodic material of the triple-meter sections.

9. Or che Giovanni

Or che Giovanni entr'al deserto esclama
E tutti chiama:
"Contriti,[a]
Fuggite,
Lasciate
Le colpe passate,
E fate penitenza, egri mortali,
Che son vicini omai gli eterni mali.

"Fuggite i prati,
Lasciate i fiori
Che sono aguati
De traditori.
Non violette,
Non fresche herbette
Che son follie,
Che son pazzie.
Alti pensieri,
Celesti imperi,
Eterne vite
Imprese grandi
Il vostro petto
Abbracci, e prenda con ogni affetto,
Ogni desio vedere Dio."

"Ahi, che bramo e desio
Vedetti, o Dio;
Ma i miei peccati
Han fatto così gran macchia al core
Che mirar non ti può, dolce Signore."

"Versa da gl'occhi
Un fonte acciocchè giunto al core
Cavi[b] la macchia del passato errore.
Così mesta e pentita un dì potrai
Gl'occhi fissar nei miei celesti rai."

Repeat of "Fuggite i prati . . ."

* * *

When he was in the wilderness John cried out
and summoned everyone:
"Contrite ones,
flee,
leave
the errors of the past,

and repent, ye feeble mortals,
for eternal evils are at hand.

"Fly from the meadows,
leave the flowers
that are the snares
of betrayers.
No sweet violets,
no fresh grasses
that are foolishness
and madness.
May your breast
embrace lofty thoughts,
heavenly kingdoms,
eternal lives,
great undertakings,
and take wholeheartedly
every desire to see God."

"Ah, how I wish and desire
to see you, O God,
but my sins
have made such a great stain upon my heart
that I am not able to look upon you, sweet Lord."

"Pour a fountain of tears from your eyes
so that, when they reach your heart
the stain of past sins is taken away.
Thus, sorrowful and penitent, you will
one day fix your eyes on my celestial rays."

Repeat of "Fly from the meadows . . ."

Note. The word marked by (a)—"Contriti"—is preceded by "Pentiti" in Anerio's setting; the word marked by (b) is "Lasci" in Anerio's setting.

Commentary. This is the only work in the *Compositioni* on a quasi-scriptural text and is appropriately labeled *spirituale*. The text may be of Roman origin; Giovanni Anerio published a setting in his *Teatro armonico spirituale* (Rome, 1619). Marini's setting comprises John the Baptist's exhortation, followed by a speech directed to God by a penitent sinner, the Deity's reply, and a repeat of the "Fuggite i prati" verse as conclusion. Anerio's setting, however, concludes with a verse not set by Marini. The Roman composer, moreover, demonstrates greater care in setting the opening lines, highlighting "esclama / E tutti chiama" before moving on to John's opening words. By contrast, Marini moves into triple meter at "E tutti chiama" and begins the Baptist's speech mid-phrase. Perhaps the most compelling moment in his setting is the canto solo "Ahi, che bramo e desio," with its close juxtapositions of *durus* and *mollis*.

10. Già brutto non son io

"Già brutto non son io se l'onda cheta
Mostrami il ver della mia vera imago,
Che mi deggia fuggir qual tigre o drago,
Colei ch'è del mio ben principio e metà.

"La fronte ho crespa, sì, ma però lieta;
Di fiamma ho 'l volto ancor, ma puro e vago,
Tal ch'arsi, il cor ne 'l tuo siringa impiago,
Di lei nel primo ciel vario pianeta.

"Dunque convien ch'in acqua io mi distempre
Mentre tutto nel foco ardo e sfavillo
Ne tu l'empio rigor, Ninfa, contempre."

"Sì," disse Pane, e bel l'amata udillo.
Non la vidd'ei, che, favellando sempre,
Fissi gl'occhi tenea nel mar tranquillo.

* * *

"I am not so ugly if still water reveals
to me my true image, which causes her
to flee from me as as from a tiger or dragon,
she who is my alpha and omega.

"My brow is furrowed, perhaps, but happy;
my face is ruddy, but pure and comely,
for I was inflamed, my heart transfixed by your syrinx,
by her, the inconstant planet in my heaven.

"Thus it is meet that I languish in water
while I burn utterly in fire and throw off sparks.
Nor can you, nymph, mitigate this harshness."

"Yes," said Pan, and well did the beloved hear him.
But he saw her not, for, ever speaking,
he kept his eyes fixed on the tranquil sea.

Commentary. The text is a difficult, obscure sonnet, possibly a trope on the eleventh idyll of Theocritus or the satyr's speech at the beginning of act 2 of Tasso's *Aminta*.[23] The speaker in all but the last three lines may be a love-smitten satyr or monsterous, Polyphemus-like figure. Marini sets the text as a strophic song with ritornelli. The continuo lines of the ritornelli and strophes 1 through 3 are not identical but very closely related. The figure that first appears at "Che mi deggia fuggir" (mm. 11–13) and the concurrent descending dotted minims on "qual tigre o drago" that serves as counterpoint are also used throughout the piece. They provide another example of Marini's reliance on sequential writing for structural extension and development (or should we say less charitably, "padding") but have little or no relevance for the text.

The somewhat unusual meter signature in the source (transcribed in this edition as $\frac{3}{4}$) may equate three semiminims in the "triple time" sections to four in the "common time" sections.[24] Thus most of the music proceeds in groups of three semiminims, but there are brief sections in four, most notably at the line " 'Sì,' disse Pane, e bel l'amata udillo." Much of the piece is in G but it briefly moves to the sharp side with a chord on E major at the end of the line of text just mentioned.

11. Or so come da sè

Or so come da sè 'l cor si disgiunge,
E come sa far pace, e guerra e tregua,
E coprir suo dolor quand'altri il punge.

Io so come in un punto si dilegua
E poi si sparge per le vene[a] il sangue
Se paura o vergogna avvien ch'il segua.

So come sta tra fior ascoso l'angue,
Come sempre fra due si voglie[b] e dorme,
Come senza timor[c] si more e langue.

xiii

***

I now know how the heart disengages from itself
and how it can make peace, wage war, and call a truce,
and conceal its sadness when others wound it.

I know how in an instant it disappears
and then blood courses through the veins
if fear or shame follow hard upon.

I know how the serpent hides in the flowers,
always between wakefulness and sleep,
and without fear it languishes and dies.

Note. Marini's text differs from commonly available editions of Petrarch[25] in a number of places; three of the most striking divergences are (a) "guance," (b) "vegghia," and (c) "languir."

Commentary. The text comprises lines 151–59 from the third part of Petrarch's *Trionfi d'amore*. They had been set by Giaches de Wert and Luca Marenzio in the previous century and as a solo song by Rasi in his *Vaghezze*.[26] Both Rasi and Marini respect the *terzetto* structure of their extracted text, the latter punctuating the verses with an instrumental ritornello. Marini's tuneful setting is a far cry from Rasi's sober, *stile recitativo,* however, and also points towards the nascent cantata genre. Marini sets the verses in diverse meters: the first and third are in triple meter while the second is in common time. The final phrase "Come senza timor si more e langue" is repeated in a coda-like finale. There is at least one affinity with "Già brutto": the repeated-note figure at the line "Dunque convien ch'in acqua io" in that work (mm. 106–13) is heard again here in the repeated iterations of "So come sta tra fior" (mm. 101–3). All three sections of this work end in C, but there is a fairly wide tonal span. Text painting ranges from the dutiful melismas on "guerra" in line 2 (m. 14ff.) to the more imaginative chromatic inflections on "dilegua" in line 4 (mm. 62 and 65).

12. *Su l'ali del tempo*

Su l'ali del tempo s'en fugge l'età
E disperde l'altrui beltà.
Eurilla gentile,
De gl'anni l'Aprile,
Purtroppo discerno
Correre al verno,
Ne indietro ritorno fa.
Su l'ali del tempo s'en fugge l'età.

La rosa, non colta
Fiorendo, langue
E 'l nativo color smari;
Ciò ch'altri si perde
Mai più si rinverde;
T'invitano l'ore,
Nunzie d'amore,
A gradir la tua beltà.
Su l'ali del tempo s'en fugge l'età.

Quel volto, che piaque
Gran tempo, s'odiò
Se color o candor mutò.
Il tempo, bifolco,
Coltiva quel solco
Cui forma il sembiante
Di vecchio amante
Che non trova in cor pietà.
Su l'ali del tempo s'en fugge l'età.

***

Age flees on the wings of time
and dissipates the beauty of others.
Charming Eurilla,
now in your springtime,
I see, nonetheless, that
your years will hasten towards winter,
and not turn back.
Age flees on the wings of time.

The rose, if unpicked
when blossoming, languishes
and loses its true color;
that which is lost
is never again renewed.
The hours,
love's messengers,
invite you to increase your beauty.
Age flees on the wings of time.

The face, which pleased for so long,
becomes hated if its innocence
or complexion is altered.
Time, that country bumpkin,
then plows that furrow
that forms the countenance
of an aged lover
who never finds sympathy in other hearts.
Age flees on the wings of time.

Commentary. The movement of time's wings is suggested by the six-minim motion. Otherwise there is little sense of text painting. The piece comprises three roughly identical strophes, each ‖: A :‖: B :‖, articulated by a ritornello. Such a description, of course, would also be perfectly apt for many of the works Marini had published nineteen years earlier in his *Scherzi e canzonette*.

13. *Spars'ho in pianto*

Spars'ho in pianto il mio sangue,
Vezzosa mia crudel,
L'alma che langue
Pur vive ancor fedel.

Tal e sua fè che mai mercè
Cercò del suo languir,
Si fidava che mai pietà
Cercò del suo morir.

Scioglie la voce il pianto
E invece sua, pur vuol
Pregarti, o bella, tanto
Ch'io miri un tanto duol.

Dal pallido sembiante
Potessi, ahi, ben mirar

S'io fossi fido amante
Quant'aspro e 'l mio penar.

Gran pena e a cor spirante
Voce impedita al dir;
Se 'l mio pur taque inante
Non taquerà i sospir.

* * *

I have shed my blood in tears,
my cruel pretty one,
yet the spirit that languishes
still lives and is faithful.

Such is its faith that never
did it seek pity while languishing,
so faithful that it never
sought pity in death.

Lamentation loosens the voice
but instead of its own it beseeches,
O fair one, that I behold
equal grief from you.

From my pale countenance
you could have well beheld
how harsh is my suffering
if I were a faithful lover.

Great suffering and expired heart,
a voice whose speech is stifled;
if mine was silent before
the sighs were not.

Commentary. Although the earliest examples of the cantata are strophic variations, by 1650 the genre had evolved into a sequence of sections variously *in stile recitativo, aria,* or *mezz'aria,* sometimes interspersed with instrumental ritornelli. In its alternation of tutti and solo sections, articulated by ritornelli, "Spars'ho in pianto," like "Io, che piansi" later in the collection, could be regarded as an example of this nascent genre. As in "Or so come da sè" there is a marked preponderance of iambic rhythm. The music does not always sound as if it is generated by the text but as if it could have been conceived independently, as illustrated by the opening duet. Both solos are technically demanding, especially the setting of "Scioglie la voce." The final section, "Gran pena e a cor spirante," recycles music from the opening.

The title in the basso partbook reads "A 5 & A 4. tralasciando questa Parte," thus indicating alternate performance as a duet for two tenors.

14. *Aure placide e volanti*

Aure placide e volanti,
Messagere del l'Aurora,
Che di rose e d'amaranti
Ingemmate il crin a Flora,
Chi di voi gli eccelsi onori
Canterà de la mia Clori?

Zeffiretti che scuotete
Vaghi fior di paradiso,
Poi ch'in ciel portato havete
Il valor di quel bel viso,
Chi dirà s'io taccio e moro
Per colei che tanto adoro?

S'io m'appresso a i lumi ardenti
Gran timor la lingua affrena,
A lei, dunque, aurette e venti,
Palesate la mia pena.[a]
Chi provò d'Amor gli strali
Muoverà più ratto l'ali.

Un dì, voi, mosso a pietade,
A lei dica i miei sospiri
Lungamente, alta beltade
Non e rea d'aspri martiri.
Chi provò d'Amor gli strali
Muoverà più ratto l'ali.

* * *

Gentle, fleeting breezes,
harbingers of dawn,
who crown Flora's tresses
with amarynths and roses,
which of you will sing the lofty honors
of my Cloris?

Little zephyrs who sway
the pretty flowers of paradise,
since you have carried to heaven
the essence of that fair face,
who shall say if I must be silent and die
for her whom I love so much?

If I draw near to the shining eyes
great fear holds back my tongue,
therefore, ye breezes and ye winds,
make known to her my sorrow.
He who has experienced love's arrows
will move his wings more quickly.

And may you, one day, moved by pity,
tell her at great length of my sighs,
for a noble beauty
is not guilty of harsh torment.
He who has experienced love's arrows
will move his wings more quickly.

Note. The line marked by (a) is "Palesate ogni mia pena" in d'India's setting.

Commentary. Settings of this text had already been published by Raffaello Rontani (Florence, 1614), by Sigismondo d'India in his *Le musiche e balli a quattro voci* (Venice: Vincenti 1621), and in Carlo Milanuzzi's *Primo scherzo delle ariose vaghezze* (Venice, 1622). Like d'India, Marini sets the four verses as a sequence of solos, but this time for different voice ranges, and he caps the work with a tutti finale. Unlike d'India he does not specifically term the piece *corrente;* nevertheless, a case could be made for such a designation.

15. *Per torbido mare*

Per torbido mare
M'ha fatto il pensiero
Di lagrime amare

Dolente nochiero.
Ma giunger in porto
Non speri mia fè
S'in poppa fortuna
Non spira per me.

Bellezze, ch'adoro
Con voglie amorose,
Di nobil tesoro
Son merci pompose.
Del arso mio core
Sospiri cocenti
Per l'onda d'amore
Son placidi venti.

* * *

Through stormy seas
the thought
of bitter tears
had made me a grief-stricken steersman.
I should not hope
to arrive in port
if fortune does not blow
favorably for me.

Beauties, which I adore
with amorous yearnings,
are but vainglorious goods
from a noble treasure.
Burning sighs
from my consumed heart
are tranquil breezes
over the waves of love.

Commentary. The gentle, six-minim motion that pervades much of the vocal sections suggests the rocking of a boat on the "torbido mare" of the suitor's tears, while the rising moan of "dolente" and the ensuing E♭–F♯ melodic interval (m. 8) are also apt pieces of text-painting. Stylistically and formally the music is cut from the same cloth as "Su l'ali del tempo."[27]

16. Io, che piansi

Io, che piansi al tuo pianto, arsi al tuo ardor[e],
Serva infelice e sconsolata amante,
Io, ch'idolo mi feci al tuo sembiante
E per dar vita a te spensi l'onore,

Or veggio e provo il tuo bugiardo core
Qual foglia al vento instabil e vagante,
Tu, lontano da me, torci le piante
Dov'hai lacci di fè frutto d'amore.

Torna, deh, torna e non voler che sia
Premio di fedelissima consorte
Il tradimento tuo, la pena mia.

Che se ne l'incostanz'ancor se forte
Sappi ch'ove pietà non mi ti dia
Darà morte a due vite una sol morte.

* * *

I, who wept at your tears, burned at your ardor,
unhappy servant and disconsolate lover,
I, who was an idol before your visage
and, in giving you life, expended my honor,

I now see and experience your false heart
as a leaf feels the uncertain, wayward wind,
you, far from me, twist the foliage
into snares for fidelity, the fruit of love.

Return, ah, return and do not wish that
a most faithful companion's reward
should be your perfidy and my suffering.

For if your inconstancy still prevails
know that if pity were not to give you back to me
it will give to two lives a single death.

Commentary. Along with "Spars'ho in pianto," "Io, che piansi" may be regarded as an early example of a cantata. The text is a sonnet set in a strophic fashion with the progression ritornello–solo–tutti–ritornello–solo–tutti. Both solo sections have elements of *recitativo* and *mez-z'aria*. The two tutti sections are not identical but closely related.

Alternate performance of the canto secondo part by a tenor is indicated in the tenor partbook ("Canto, o Tenore"), while another alternative, to use two tenors in place of the cantos, is indicated in the basso and basso continuo partbooks ("due Canti, o Tenori").

17. Una fanciulla

Una fanciulla m'ha rubato il cor.
M'ha privo di libertà
Questa cruda d'Amor.
Son preso, son legato, io moro.
E pur questa crudel non vol udir
I miei sospir, i miei dolor.

Una fanciulla m'ha ferito il sen.
E non trovo, ohimè, pietà
Quanto più vengo men.
Son punto, son piagato, io spiro.
E pur la cruda ogn'or priva di fè,
Nega mercè, mi dà velen.

* * *

A girl has stolen my heart.
Love's cruel one has deprived
me of freedom.
I'm taken, bound, and I die.
And yet this cruel one does not wish
to hear my sighs and my pains.

A girl has wounded my bosom.
And I find, alas, no compassion
no matter how much I grow faint.
I'm stung, I'm wounded, and I expire.
And yet the cruel one, bereft of faith,
denies me mercy, and poisons me.

Commentary. As in "Su l'ali del tempo," the text and music of the opening line of each strophe is repeated at the end of the strophe, both strophes articulated by brief instrumental ritornelli. A final coda extends and emphasizes "m'ha ferito il sen." The piece is the simplest of the collection; a "pop song" perhaps, akin to the *alla Venetiana* pieces in Marini's opp. 2 and 3.

18. Addio begl'occhi

Addio begl'occhi, addio stelle serene,
Cagion delle mie pene,
Poichè quando vi miro
Verso lagrime ogn'ora sospiro.
Voglio da voi partire
Ch'io non posso mirarvi e non morire.

* * *

Farewell beautiful eyes, farewell serene stars,
cause of my sorrows,
for when I look upon you
I constantly shed tears and sigh.
I wish to depart from you,
for I cannot look upon you and not die.

Commentary. This concluding work is the only piece in the collection scored for more than three singing voices. The topic appropriately concerns departure and farewell. The text is short, yet its six lines are drawn out at length with a great amount of word and phrase repetition, hearkening back to the concerto idiom of opus 7.

The opening section is marked by an obsessive rocking bass that comes to three successive halts, cadencing on D, C, and G, respectively. Consecutive seconds contribute an edgy flavor, as does the drawn-out half cadence on "pene" (mm. 31–33). The line "Poichè quando vi miro" initiates a new section, with the subsequent line "ogn'ora il sospiro" sung to short broken figures, mirroring the repetitions of "Addio" in the opening section. The final section begins in measure 96 and is centered on drawn-out pedal points, successively on A, D, G, and C. The phrase "e non morire" is sung in long values that contrast with the short figures of "non posso mirarvi."

Notes

1. Bayerisches Hauptstaatsarchiv, Geheimes Hausarchiv Akt. Nr. 2508, Personenselekt Karton 232/Marini. Transcriptions and translations of the document may be found in Willene Clark, "The Vocal Music of Biagio Marini" (Ph.D. diss., Yale University, 1966), 1:38 and 255–56, and Georg Brunner, *Biagio Marini: Die Revolution in der Instrumentalmusik* (Schrobenhausen: Verlag Bickel, 1997), 138–39. Clark conjectures that the letter was intended for both Duke Albrecht of Bavaria and his brother Ferdinand, archibishop of Cologne. In the letter Marini was apparently offering himself for employment at the Bavarian court.

2. A collection of sacred music entitled *Viridarium musicum* was published in Neuburg in 1628, the year of Marini's departure. It includes two pieces by musicians who worked under him at the Neuburg court, one of whom was Matthew Blüm, who had preceded Marini as kapellmeister there. The collection apparently no longer survives but is described in Robert Eitner, *Bibliographie der Musik-Sammelwerke des XVI. und XVII. Jahrhunderts* (reprint, Hildesheim: Olms, 1963), 278. It is interesting that no works by Marini were included.

3. Brescia, Archivio di Stato, ASC Polizze 28/bis, busta 212 and ASC 28/bis, busta 83; and Catasto Antico Registro 3. The documents were discovered by Maura Zoni. According to the documents, Marini rented part of a house to a Gio Batta Chizola. See Biagio Marini, *Sonate sinfonie: Canzoni, passemezzi, bulletti, correnti, gagliarde, & ritornelli, a 1, 2, 3, 4, 5 & 6 voci per ogni sorte di stromento, opera VIII*, ed. Maura Zoni, Monumenti musicali italiani, vol. 23 (Milan: Suvini Zerboni, 2003), vi–viii.

4. Archivio Veneranda Fabbrica Duomo, OC, 30; noted in Robert Kendrick, *The Sounds of Milan, 1585–1650* (Oxford: Oxford University Press, 2002), 35.

5. Davide Daolmi, *Le Origini dell'opera a Milano (1598–1649)* (Turnhout: Brepols, 1998), 339.

6. From a document discovered by Stephen Bonta, cited in Eleanor Selfridge-Field, *Venetian Instrumental Music from Gabrieli to Vivaldi*, 3rd rev. ed. (New York: Dover, 1994), 152. In 1648 Marini applied for the position of *maestro di capella* at the Basilica of Santa Maria Maggiore in Bergamo. The position was awarded to Filippo Vitali. See Maurizio Padoan, "Legrenzi a Santa Maria Maggiore," in Francesco Passadore and Franco Rossi, eds., *Giovanni Legrenzi e la capella ducale di San Marco* (Florence: Olschki, 1994), 12.

7. See Roark Miller, "Divorce, Dismissal, but No Disgrace: Biagio Marini's Career Revisited," *Recercare* 9 (1997): 16.

8. Approximate ages of his children by Helena Hanin are also given in later Brescian *polizze d'estime* from 1653 and 1660. For a transcription of the 1641 document see Fabio Fano, "Nuovi documenti e appunti su Biagio Marini," *Scritti in onore di Luigi Ronga* (Milan: Riccardo Ricciardi, 1973), 148–50. For the latter two see Paolo Guerrini, "Per la storia della musica a Brescia," *Note d'archivio per la storia musicale* 11, no. 1 (1934): 16–17.

9. Clark ("The Vocal Music of Biagio Marini," 1:42) states that he was mentioned "as Music Director in Düsseldorf" in a letter from 1640, citing as her source Wilibald Nagel, "Gilles Heine," *Monatshefte für Musikgeschichte* 28 (1896): 95. This has been disputed as a misreading, however, in Aurelio Bianco, Emilie Corswarem, and Philippe Vendrix, "Gilles Hayne, Biagio Marini et le Duc de Neuburg," *Studi musicali* 36 (2007): 384 n. 73.

10. At least one member of Scaglia's family was a patron of the arts. A Cardinal Desiderio Scaglia (d. 1639) was the dedicatee of Frescobaldi's *Canzoni da sonare a una due tre, et quattro con il basso continuo . . . libro primo* (Venice, 1634). See Daniele Torelli, "Sopra le tenebre del mio povero inchiostro: Biagio Marini e la musica sacra," in *La musica e il sacro, atti del XI Convegno internazionale sul barocco padano nei secoli XVII–XVIII* (Como: AMIS, 2003), 155 n. 27.

11. Although Marini worked with stanzaic texts in some of the *concerti* in his opus 7, only the last two in that collection have instrumental interludes. The term "dance song" is even more viable when applied to some of the works in Marini's opus 16, which appeared eight years later. In that print he explicitly terms some pieces "corrente" or "concerto con corrente."

12. A typical example is Chiabrera's "Fugge'l verno de' dolori" set by Monteverdi in his *Scherzi musicali a tre voci* of 1607.

13. According to John Whenham, the use of refrain and rondo structures in the duet began in the 1630s. See Whenham, *Duet and Dialogue in the Age of Monteverdi* (Ann Arbor: UMI, 1982), 1:218ff.

14. A text of similar line lengths is given by Silke Leopold in the chapter "Die Tradition der Villanelle," in *Al modo d'Orfeo: Dichtung und Musik im italienischen Sologesang des frühen 17. Jahrhunderts,* Analecta Musicologica 29, vol. 1 (Laaber: Laaber Verlag, 1995), 207.

15. Attribution from Repertorio della Poesia Italiana in Musica, 1500–1700, http://repim.muspe.unibo.it, database edited by Angelo Pompilio, University of Bologna, Department of Music and Theater; accessed on 30 October 2009. Modern edition in Gianfrancesco Maia Materdona di Mesagne, *Opere,* ed. Gino Rizzo (Lecce: Milella, 1989), 100.

16. Modern edition by Glenn Watkins in Sigismondo d'India, *Il terzo libro dei madrigali a cinque voci (1615),* Musiche rinascimentali siciliane, vol. 15 (Florence: Olschki, 1995), 45–47.

17. Facsimile reproduction in *Eastern Po Valley,* ed. Gary Tomlinson, Italian Secular Song, 1606–1636, vol. 5 (New York: Garland, 1986), 166–67.

18. This is one of only two instances in Marini's extant music in which this well-known *seicento* device is used. The other is in the *Miserere III* in his *Lacrime di Davide sparse nel miserere,* opus 21, published in 1655. For a general discussion of this device see Ellen Rosand, "The Descending Tetrachord: An Emblem of Lament," *Musical Quarterly* 55 (1979): 346–59.

19. Attribution from Repertorio della Poesia Italiana in Musica, 1500–1700, ed. Pompilio; accessed on 30 October 2009. Modern edition in Materdona, *Opere,* 154.

20. The beginning of the third stanza illustrates Marini's thinking in musical terms at the expense of the text: the close canon between the voices may be interesting musically, but the lengthening of the final syllable of "crudele" is questionable.

21. The text may be found at http://www.bibliotecaitaliana.it/repository/bibit/bibit001304/bibit001304.xml.

22. The second section, comprising lines 5–8, begins in measure 69 and is labeled "Finale" in the source. The division of the poem into two four-line verses was also adopted by Pietro Benedetti in his much simpler setting for solo voice printed in his *Musiche libro secondo* (Venice, 1613).

23. Specifically lines 34–44 of act 2, scene 1.

24. This meter signature is discussed by Johann Peter Sperling in his *Principia musicae* (Bautzen, 1700). He states that it was used by seventeenth-century German violinists. See George Houle, *Meter in Music, 1600–1800: Performance, Perception, and Notation* (Bloomington: Indiana University Press, 1987), 43–45.

25. Such as the one presented at http://digilander.libero.it/letteratura_petrarca/petrarca_i_trionfi.html.

26. Wert and Marenzio include the lines 148–50 beginning "Dura legge d'Amor." Wert's setting is in his *Madrigali del fiore* (Venice, 1561); Marenzio's in his *Il nono libro de madrigali* (Venice, 1599). A facsimile of Rasi's setting is in Tomlinson, *Eastern Po Valley,* 183–84.

27. As in "Spars'ho in pianto," the ritornello proceeds in semiminims and dotted minims while those vocal sections that are in triple meter move in semibreves and minims. See the critical notes.

Plates

CANTO ò Tenore, ouero Alto
COMPOSITIONI VARIE
PER MVSICA DI CAMERA
A Due, Tre, Quattro, Cinque, Voci, e parte con due Violini
DEDICATE
All'Illustrissimo, & Reuerendissimo Signor il Signor
D. VALERIANO SCAGLIA
ABBATE GENERALE DELL'ORDINE OLIVETANO
DA BIAGIO MARINI
Gentil'huomo, & Cauagliere del Sereniss. Palatino di Noiburg.
OPERA DECIMATERZA·

IN VENETIA,
Apresso Alessandro Vincenti. MDCXXXXI.

Plate 1. Biagio Marini, *Compositioni varie per musica di camera*, opus 13 (1641), Canto ò Tenore, overo Alto partbook, title page (shelf mark 50600 Muz. UNIKAT). Courtesy of Biblioteka Uniwersytecka, Wrocław, Poland.

Plate 2. Biagio Marini, *Compositioni varie per musica di camera,* opus 13 (1641), Tenore partbook, "Qui, dove il sol," measures 39–91 (shelf mark 50600 Muz. UNIKAT). Note the insertion of measures 69–70 in the bottom right of the page, which are missing above. Courtesy of Biblioteka Uniwersytecka, Wrocław, Poland.

*Compositioni varie
per musica di camera*

Opus 13

Dedication

ILLUSTRISSIMO E Reverendissimo Signore, Patron Colendissimo,

La Musica di sua natura ordinata a dar gusto altrui, e di colui che più la gradisce, & a cui più diletta; in quella guisa che la robba senza Padrone e di chi primiero se la occupa. Queste compositioni sono di V.S. Illustrissima, e Reverendissima; havendole io fatte, acciò che piacciano a lei, si come e succeduto per mia fortuna, e per sua gentilezza. Si che nel darle alla Stampa non glile dedico come mie, ma gliele presento come sue: e però non mi conosco in necessita di pregarlo, che voglia protegerle. E ben vero che la parte, che ho in esse, come efficiente; desidero mi sia computata, per dimostratione de' molti miei obblighi, e per segnale dell'infinita mia osservanza, verso di Lei, e di tutta l'Illustrissima Casa, alla qual prego continuate exaltationi, e reverentissimo le bacio le mani.

Di V.S. Illustrissima, e Reverendissima. Di Venetia li 23. Genaro 1641.

Most illustrious and most reverend lord, warmest patron,

Music is ordained by its nature to give pleasure to others. The more someone appreciates it the greater delight it will grant, and in such a manner he becomes the first owner of goods that initially are without one. These compositions belong to Your Most Illustrious and Reverend Lordship. I have made them in order that they please him, if, through my good fortune and his kindness, they succeed. If I publish them, I do not dedicate them as being mine, but present them to him as his own. Therefore I know no necessity to ask him to protect them, and truly the effective part I have in them I desire to be viewed as a demonstration of my many obligations, and as an indication of my infinite observance towards Him and towards his entire illustrious house which, I pray, will be continually exalted. And I most reverently kiss the hands of Your Most Illustrious and Reverend Lordship. Venice, the 23rd of January 1641.

1. Torna l'inverno, frigido

*The two canto parts can also be sung by two tenors an octave lower.

Che d'o- gni tem- po nel mio pet- to, che d'o- gni tem- po nel mio pet- to du- pet- to, che d'o- gni tem- po nel mio pet- to du- -ra. Gli ar- bo- scel- li si spo- -ra. Gli ar- bo- scel- li si spo- -do- -glia- no Del fron- -do- -glia- no Del fron- -do- -so ve- stir, -do- -so, del fron- do- so ve- stir,

34
Par ch'i pra- ti si do- glia- no Che più non puon fio- rir, Che più non
Par ch'i pra- ti si do- glia- no Che più non puon fio- rir, che
39
puon fio- rir, Che più non puon fio- rir, non puon
più non puon fio- rir, che più non puon fio- rir, non puon
43
fio- rir; Ma nel- l'ar- so mio co- re
fio- rir;
48
Sem-pre più cre- sce e si rin- for- za a- mo- re,
Ma nel- l'ar- so mio co- re Sem- pre più cre- sce e si rin-

Sempre più cresce e si rinforza, sempre più cresce e si rinforza amore.

-forza, sempre più cresce e si rinforza amore. Le nevi i monti altissimi Già fanno biancheggiar E da giacci durissimi Coperto il tutto par; Ma l'amo-

Le nevi i monti altissimi Già fanno biancheggiar E da giacci durissimi Coperto il tutto par;

68
-ro- so fo- co Spe- gner non puo- te in me ne tem- po o lo- co,
Ma l'a- mo- ro- so fo- co
♯ ♯ ♯
72
Spe- gner non puo- te in me ne tem- po, spe- gner non puo- te in me ne tem- po o
Spe- gner non puo- te in me ne tem- po, spe- gner non puo- te in me ne tem- po o
♯5
76
lo- co. A ven- ti, a ven-
lo- co. A ven- ti, a
♯ ♯ ♮
80
ti che ga- reg- gia- no, ga- reg-
ven- ti che ga- reg- gia- no, ga-

83
-reg-
87
- gia- no Co 'l cal- do so- spi- rar, A
- gia- no Co 'l cal- do so- spi- rar,
5 6 # 6 # (♯)5
91
piog- ge, a piog- ge, a piog- ge, a
A piog- ge, a piog- ge, a piog-
94
piog- ge, a piog- ge, a piog- ge
- ge, a piog- ge, a piog- ge, a piog-

97
che pa- reg- gia- no Il lun- go la-
ge che pa- reg- gia- no Il lun- go la-
101
gri- mar, Veg- gio che vien l'in- ver- no, Ma que- sto pas- sa e il mio
gri- mar,
106
re- sta e- ter- no, Ma ques- to pas- sa e il mio
Veg- gio che vien l'in- ver- no, Ma que- sto pas- sa e il mio re- sta,
110
re- sta, ma que- sto pas- sa e il mio re- sta e- ter- no.
ma que- sto pas- sa e il mio re- sta e- ter- no.

2. Ecco ch'io manco

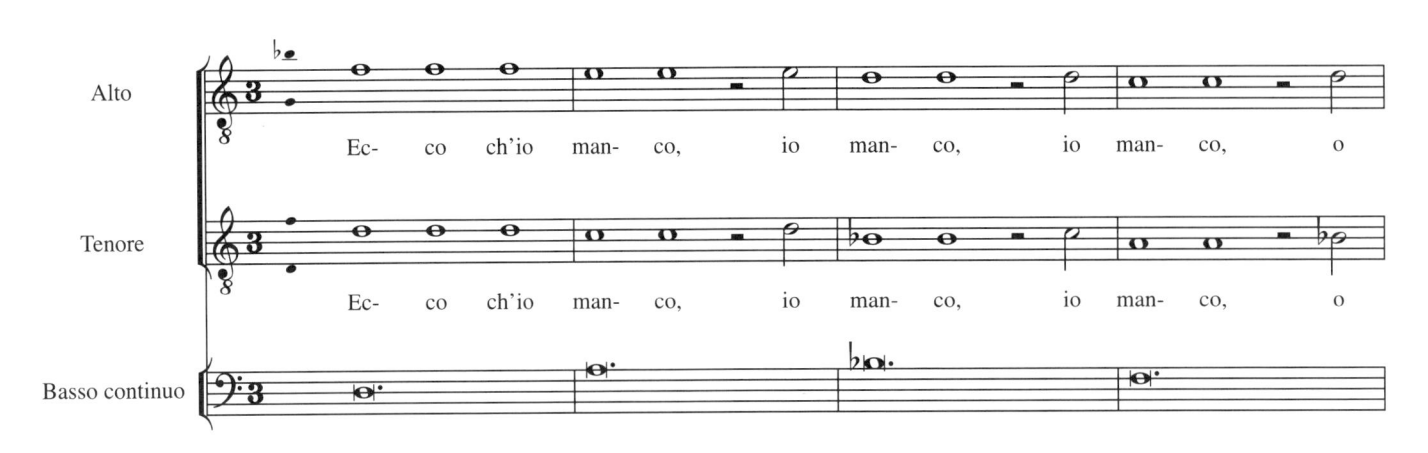

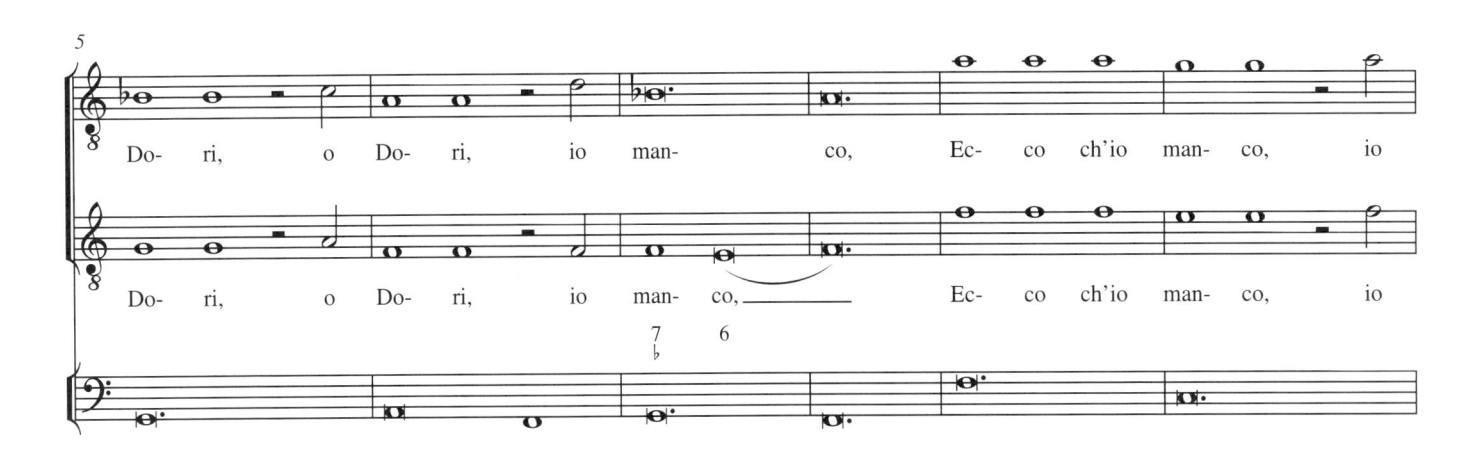

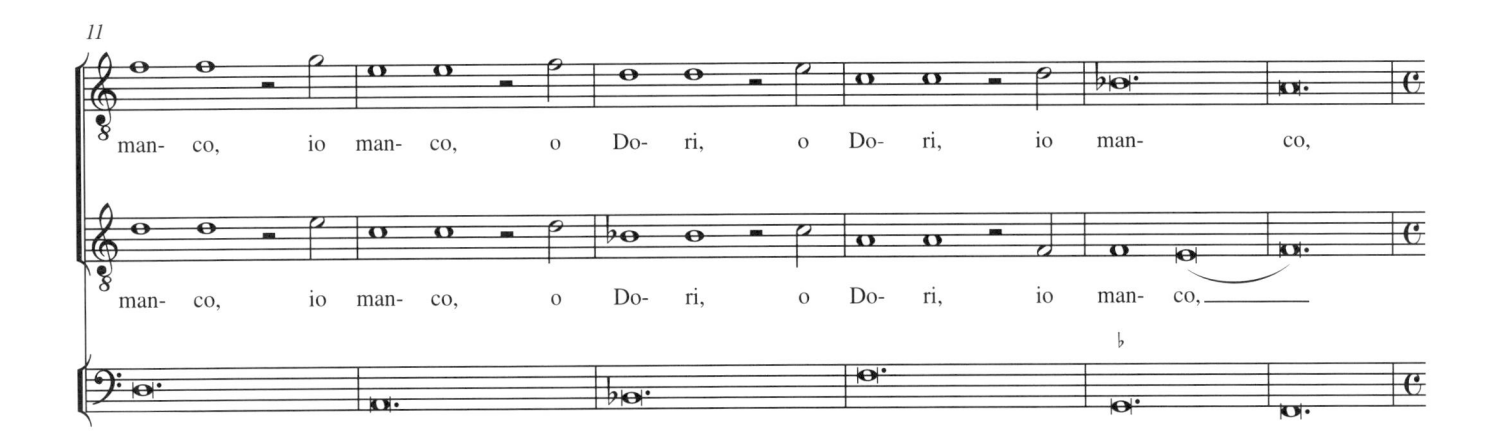

11

43
pur, in- fe- del, Qual- che ri- sto-
49
Qual- che ri- sto- ro.
-ro, Qual- che ri- sto- ro.
54
Per- fi- da, per- fi- da, per- fi- da, e co- sì,
Per- fi- da, per- fi- da, per- fi- da,
59
per- fi- da, per- fi- da, e co- sì, co- sì sti- mai il
e co- sì, e co- sì, co- sì sti- mai il

vi- ver mi- o, Per- fi- da, per- fi- da, e co- sì,

vi- ver mi- o, Per- fi- da, per- fi- da,

per- fi- da, per- fi- da, e co- sì, co- sì sti- mai il

e co- sì, e co- sì, co- sì sti- mai il

vi- ver mi- o! Ad- dio bel- tà cru- del, Io mo- ro, ad- di- o.

vi- ver mi- o! Ad- dio bel- tà cru-

Ad- dio bel- tà cru- del, Io mo- ro, ad- di- o. Ad- dio bel- tà cru- del, ad-

-del, Io mo- ro, ad- di- o. Ad- dio bel- tà cru- del, Io mo- ro, ad- di- o. Io mo- ro,

85
-di- o, ad-di- o, ad- di- o, ad-di- o, ad- di- o, ad-di- o, ad- di- o, ad- di- o, Ad-
mo- ro, mo- ro, mo- ro, Ad-
89
-dio bel- tà cru- del, Io mo- ro, mo- ro, mo- ro, Ad-
-dio bel- tà cru- del, ad- di- o, ad- di- o, ad- di- o, ad-di- o, Ad-
93
-dio bel- tà cru- del, Io mo- ro, io mo- ro, ad- di- o, ad- di- o.
-dio bel- tà cru- del, Io mo- ro, io mo- ro, ad- di- o, ad- di- o.

3. Miratemi o begl'occhi

*The two alto parts can also be sung by two cantos a fifth higher; the basso continuo part would then be transposed down a fourth.

U- na vi- sta gen- til poi me la ren- de, U- na vi- sta gen-
vi- ta un fier de- si- o U- na vi- sta gen- til, u- na vi- sta gen- til poi me la ren-

-til, u- na vi- sta gen- til, u- na vi- sta gen- til poi me la ren- de.
-de, U- na vi- sta gen- til, u- na vi- sta gen- til poi me la ren- de.

Mi- ra- te- mi, mi- ra- te- mi o be-
Mi- ra- te- mi, mi- ra- te- mi, mi- ra- te- mi o be-

-gl'oc- chi, o qual sen- t'i- o, o qual sen- t'i- o Gio-
-gl'oc- chi, qual sen- t'i- o

- ia per voi, qual sen- t'i- o, qual sen- t'i- o

Gio- - ia per voi, qual sen- t'i- o gio-

- gio- - ia per voi, per voi che al- l'a- ni- ma s'ap-

- ia per voi, per voi, per voi che al-

-pren- de, Si spa- zia fuor di sè lo spir- to mi- o,

-l'a- ni- ma s'ap- pren- de, Si spa- zia fuor di sè lo spir- to mi- o, Si spa- zia fuor di

si spa- zia fuor di sè Quan- do 'l bel vo- stro lu- me al cor, al cor, al

sè lo spir- to mi- o Quan- do 'l bel vo- stro lu- me al cor, al cor,

50
cor, al cor mi scen- de. Mi- ra- te- mi‿o be- gl'oc-
al cor mi scen- de. Mi- ra- te- mi‿o be- gl'oc- chi,
6
54
chi, un dol- ce gi- - ro Se ri- vol- ge- te‿in me, un dol- ce gi-
un dol- ce gi- - ro Se ri- vol- ge- te‿in
(♭)
57
- ro se ri- vol- ge- te‿in me, se ri- vol- ge- te‿in me, mi sol- le- va-
me, un dol- ce gi- - ro se ri- vol- ge- te‿in me,
61
- te Dal cie- co‿a- bis- - so al lu- mi- no-
al lu- mi- no-

19

83
-ra- te- mi o be- gl'oc- chi,
-mi, mi- ra- - te- mi o be- gl'oc- chi,
(♭)
88
e di lei per cui so- spi- ro Tem- pri la cru-del- tà vo-
e di lei per cui so- spi- ro Tem- pri la cru-del- tà
92
- stra pie- ta- te, vo- - stra pie- ta- te.
vo- stra pie- ta- te, vo- stra pie- ta- te.
♯ 6 ♯ 6

4. Deh, come in un momento

13
Co- me si to- sto giun- ge Il do- lor, il do- lor che mi pun-
Co- me si to- sto giun- ge Il do- lor, il do- lor che mi pun-
Il do- lor che mi pun-
6
18
-ge E chi da gl'oc- chi
-ge Su l'in- ti- mo del co- re, E chi da gl'oc- chi fo-
-ge E chi da gl'oc- chi fo-
24
fo- re Mi trae di pian- to‿un ma- -
-re Mi trae di pian- to‿un ma-
-re Mi trae di pian- to‿un ma-

29
-re, un ma- - - re, E
- re, un ma- - - re,
- - - - re,
34
d'a- spre pe- ne‿a- ma- re M'in- gom- - bra l'al-
E d'a- spre
E d'a- spre
39
- ma‿e 'l se- no, E d'a- spre pe- ne‿a-
pe- ne‿a- ma- re M'in- gom- - bra l'al- - ma‿e 'l
pe- ne‿a- ma- re, E d'a- spre pe- ne

44
-ma- re M'in- gom- - bra l'al-
se- no, M'in- gom-
M'in- gom- - bra l'al- ma e 'l
48
-ma e 'l se- no. Ah, ch'in un ba-
- bra il se- no. Ah, ah voi, ch'in un ba- le- no,
se- no. Ah,
♯
52
-le- no, Oc- chi mi da- te se- gno Che v'an- noi mi- a
Tur- ba- ti di di- sde- gno,
ah,
7 [♯]6 5 6

56
vi- ta, E che da voi spa- ri- ta Sia que- sta lu- ce on- d'i- o
6
60
Ar- - - - do,
Ar- - - - do,
Ar- - - - do,
6 6
64
ar- do, ar- do di bel de- si- o, di bel de- si- o,
ar- do, ar- do di bel de- si- o, di bel de- si-
ar- do, ar- do, ar- - do, ar- do, ar- do, ar-
6

68
Ar- do, ar- - do, ar- do, ar- do di bel de-
-o, Ar- do, ar- do, ar- - do, ar- do di bel de-
-do di bel de- si- o, di bel de- si- o, di bel de-
72
-si- o. Non da- te al mio fal- li- re Co- tan- to di mar-
-si- o. Non da- te al mio fal- li- re
-si- o. Non da- te al mio fal- li- re
77
-ti- re. Non pos- sa fe- ri- ta- te, Pie- ta- te, ohi-mè, pie-
Pie- ta- te, ohi- mè, pie- ta- te, Non pos- sa fe- ri- ta- te, Non pos- sa fe- ri-
Pie- ta- te, ohi-mè, pie- ta- te,
6

27

-ta- te, Nel vo- stro bel se- re- no;

-ta- te Nel vo- stro bel se- re- no; Ma voi, be- a- ti a pie- no Con vo-

Nel vo- stro bel se- re- no;

Be- a- te, be- a- te, be- a- te, be- a- te gl'al- trui co- ri,

-str'al- mi splen- do- ri, Be- a-

Be- a- te, be-

Be- a- te, be- a- te, be- a- te gl'al- trui co- ri.

-te, be- a- te, be- a- te gl'al- trui co - ri.

-a- te, be- a- te, be- a- te gl'al- trui co- ri.

5. Qui, dove il sol

11
cie- lo in un co 'l ciel le men- ti, E͜ i pa- sto- rel- li͜ i lor ca- no-
cie- lo in un co 'l ciel le men- ti, E͜ i pa- sto- rel- li͜ i lor ca- no-
E͜ i pa- sto- rel- li͜ i lor ca- no-
16
-ri ac- cen- - ti, i lor ca- no- - ri͜ ac- cen-
-ri ac- cen- ti, i lor ca- no- - ri͜ ac- cen-
-ri ac- cen- ti, i lor ca- no- - ri͜ ac- cen-
6
[♯]6
22
-ti De- star di pog- - gio͜ in pog- gio, de- star di
-ti De- star di pog- gio͜ in pog- gio, de- star di pog- gio͜ in pog-
-ti De- star di pog- gio͜ in pog- - gio, de- star di pog- gio͜ in

pog- gio in pog- - gio han per co- stu- - me,

-gio han per co- stu- - - me,

pog- gio per co- - stu- - me,

Qui, do- ve il mon- te om- breg- gia on- deg- gia il fiu-

-me, in- cre- span l'au- re i ven- ti, i

Rin- fre- scan l'om- bra in- cre- span l'au- re i ven- ti, i ven-

ven- - ti,

-ti, Son- don l'her- bet- te i man- su- e-

46
A
T
B
B.c.
Spie- gan gli‿au-gei le la- sci- vet- te piu- me,
- ti‿ar- men- ti, Spie- gan gli‿au- gei le la- sci- vet- te
Spie- gan gli‿au- gei le la- sci- vet- te piu- me, le la- sci- vet- te
7 [♯]6 ♯
50
Spie- gan gli‿au- gei le la- sci- vet- te piu- me, le la- sci- vet- te piu- me, le
piu- me, Spie- gan gli‿au- gei le la- sci- vet- te piu- me,
piu- me, le la- sci- vet- te piu- me, Spie- gan gli‿au- gei le
7 [♯]6 7 6
54
la- sci- vet- te piu- me, le la- sci- vet- te piu- me, Qui, do- ve‿i
Spie- gan gli‿au- gei le la- sci- vet- te piu- me, Qui, do- ve‿i
la- sci- vet- te piu- me, Qui, do- ve‿i
6

pu- ri e tra- spa- ren- ti u- mo- ri Fan- no spec- chio a le fron- de e 'l

pu- ri e tra- spa- ren- ti u- mo- ri Fan- no spec- chio a le fron- de e 'l

pu- ri e tra- spa- ren- ti u- mo- ri

A: bel ter- re- no, Tut- to, tut- to, tut- to spi- ra de- li- zie,

T: bel ter- re- no, Tut- to, tut- to, tut- to spi- ra de- li- zie,

B.c.

spi- ra de- li- zie e tut- to a- mo- ri,

spi- ra de- li- zie e tut- to a- mo- ri, Qui vie- ni,

Qui vie- ni, vie- ni, o Cin-

vie- ni, o Cin- tia, vie- ni, vie- ni in que- sto si- to a- me- no,

33

98
vie- ni, vie- ni, o Cin- tia, Cor- re- mo
vie- ni, vie- ni, o Cin- tia, Cor- re- mo
si- to, in que- sto si- to a- me- no; Cor- re- mo, cor-
103
io dol- ci frut- ti,
io dol- ci frut- ti, io dol- ci
-re- mo io dol- ci frut- ti e tu, e tu, io dol- ci frut- ti, io
7 [♯]6 7 6 7 [♯]6
108
io dol- ci frut- ti, io dol- ci frut- ti, io dol- ci frut- ti e tu bei
frut- ti, io dol- ci frut- ti, io dol- ci frut- ti e tu bei fio- ri, io dol- ci frut- ti,
dol- ci frut- ti e tu bei fio- ri, io dol- ci frut- ti, io dol- ci

111

fio- ri, io dol- ci frut- ti e tu bei fio- ri, io dol- ci frut- ti, io dol- ci

io dol- ci frut- ti, io dol- ci frut- ti, io dol- ci frut- ti e tu bei fio- ri, io

frut- ti, io dol- ci frut- ti, io dol- ci frut- ti,

114

frut- ti e tu bei fio- ri,

dol- ci frut- ti e tu bei fio- ri, Tu nel bel pra- to ed

io dol- ci frut- ti e tu bei fio- ri,

118

Tu nel bel pra- to ed io, ed io nel tuo bel

io, ed io nel tuo bel se- no, Tu nel bel pra- to ed

Tu nel bel pra- to, tu nel bel pra- to, tu nel bel pra- to,

122
se- no, Tu nel bel pra- to ed io, ed io nel tuo bel
io, ed io nel tuo bel se- no, Tu nel bel pra- to ed
tu nel bel pra- to, tu nel bel pra- to, tu nel bel
126
se- no, nel tuo bel se- no, ed io, ed io,
io, ed io nel tuo bel se- no, Tu nel bel pra- to ed io, ed
pra- to ed io, ed io, ed io, ed io nel tuo bel
130
Tu nel bel pra- to ed io, ed io nel tuo bel se- no.
io, ed io nel tuo bel se- - no.
se- no, ed io, ed io nel tuo bel se- no.

6. Pastorella

17
B
-la, Non par- ti- re, Non par- ti- re, Non fug- gi- re, Non par-
6
B.c.
22
-ti- re, Non par- ti- re, Non par- ti- re, Non fug- gi- re, Che se fug- gi, se fug-
26
- gi, se fug- - gi, se fug- - gi Tu mi
7
[♭]6
30
Ritornello
Vn. 1
Vn. 2
B
strug- gi.
[5]
B.c.
34
Vn. 1
Vn. 2
B.c.

38
42
Vn. 1
Vn. 2
C
B.c.
Tor- na, tor- na Fac- cia a- dor- na, Por- gi a- i- ta,
46
Che la vi- ta Di te pri- va Non e vi- va, Por- gi a- i- ta, Che la vi- ta Di te
50
pri- va, Por- gi a- i- ta, Por- gi a- i- ta, Che la vi- ta Di te pri- va Non e
54
vi- va, Por- gi a- i- ta, Che la vi- ta Di te pri- va Non e vi-

Ritornello
Vn. 1
Vn. 2
C
B.c.
-va.
Vn. 1
Vn. 2
B.c.
Vn. 1
Vn. 2
C
B
B.c.
Ma, cru- de-
Ma, cru-
C
B
B.c.
-le, Le que- re- le Sde- gni in- tan- to; Del mio pian- to,
-de- le, Le que- re- le Sde- gni in- tan- to; Del mio pian-

75
— Ma, cru- de- le, Le que- re- le, Le que- re- le
-to, Ma, cru- de- le, Le que- re- le Sde- gni in- tan-
6 6 5
79
Sde- gni in- tan- to; Del mio pian- to, Sde- gni in- tan-
-to; Del mio pian- - to, Sde- gni in- tan- to; Del mio
6
83
-to; Del mio pian- to Non ri- spon- di, Pur t'a- scon- di, Non ri- spon- di, Pur t'a-
pian- to Non ri- spon- di, Pur t'a- scon- - di, Non ri- spon- di,
87
-scon- di, Non ri- spon- di, Pur t'a- scon- di,
Pur t'a- scon- - di, Non ri- spon- di, Pur t'a- scon-

Non ri- spon- di, Pur t'a- scon- di, Non ri- spon- di, Pur t'a- scon- di, Non ri- spon- di, Pur t'a- scon- di,

Ritornello

Non ri- spon- di, Pur t'a- scon- di.

43

S'hai pur gio- ia Ch'io mi moi-

Ritornello

-a;

Finale a 4

Che go-

Che go-

-dra- i Che ve- dra- i

-dra- i Che ve- dra- i Da la sal- ma Par- tir

l'al- - - -

-ma Per ser- vir- ti, Per gra- dir- ti, Per ser- vir- ti, Per ser- vir- ti,

46

7. Non fuggir, vago augello

-lo, Che non ten- do a tuoi dan- ni o vi- sco o_ re-

-lo,

-te; Che s'a me li- ber- tà cer- co e qui- e- te,

Por- te non deg-gio in ser- vi- tu- te e'n duo- lo.

Ben io fug- go, io fug- go, io fug- go, fug- go a ra- -gion ne- mi- co stuo- lo Di gra- vi cu- re in que- st'om- bre se- cre- te, O- ve sol per go- der, si- cu- re e lie- te, Po- ch'o- re te- co, al- la cit- tà, al- la cit- tà m'in- vo- lo.

Qui più sereno è il ciel, più l'aria pura, Più dolci l'acque, e più cortese e bella L'alte richezze sue scopre natura.

52
O men- te͜ u- ma- na,
O men- te͜ u- ma- na, al pro- prio ben, al pro- prio ben ru- bel-
58
A
T
B.c.
al pro-prio ben, al pro-prio ben ru- bel- la!
-la, O men- te͜ u- ma- na,
64
Ve- de tan- ta sua pa- ce e non la cu-
Ve- de tan- ta sua pa- ce͜ e non la cu- ra,
69
-ra, E sti- ma por- to͜ ov' ha flut- - to, flut- to͜ e pro- cel- la,
E sti- ma por- to͜ ov' ha flut- to, flut- to͜ e pro- cel-

73
E sti- ma por- to͜ ov' ha flut- to, flut- to͜ e pro- cel-
- la, E sti- ma por- to͜ ov' ha flut- - to, flut- to͜ e pro-
76
Vn. 1
Vn. 2
A
- la, pro- cel- la, E sti- ma
T
-cel- la,
B.c.
80
por- to͜ ov' ha flut- - to, flut- to͜ e pro- cel-
E sti- ma por- to͜ ov' ha flut- to, flut- to͜ e pro- cel-

53

8. Che non senta per voi

che non sen- ta per voi tor- men- ti e gua- i, Ch'il cor non mi con-
Che non sen- ta per voi

-su- mi a- spro ve- le- no, Ch'il cor non mi con- su- mi, ch'il
tor- men- ti e gua- i, Ch'il cor non mi con- su- mi a- spro ve-

cor non mi con- su- mi a- spro ve- le- no,
-le- no, Ch'il cor non mi con- su- mi, ch'il cor non mi con- su- mi a- spro ve-

Ch'io non a- do- ri i vo- stri dol- ci ra- i, Ch'io non a- do-
-le- no, Ch'io non a- do-

-ri i vo- stri dol- ci ra- i, Ch'io non a- do- ri, ch'io non a-
-ri i vo- stri dol- ci ra- i, Ch'io non a- do- ri, ch'io non a- do- ri,

42
Vn. 1
Vn. 2
A
-do- ri i vo- stri dol- ci ra- i, Ch'io non a- do- ri, ch'io
B
ch'io non a- do- ri, ch'io non a- do-
B.c.
46
non a- do- ri i vo- - stri dol- ci ra- i, Ch'io non sia di de-
-ri i vo- stri dol- ci ra- i,
50
-sir e d'a- mor pie- - no,
Ch'io non sia di de- sir e d'a- mor pie- no,

Ritornello di sopra
Vn. 1
Vn. 2
B.c.
Finale a 4
A
B
Che in que- ste brac- cia A- mor vi strin- ga ma- i,
Che in que- ste brac- cia A- mor vi strin- ga ma- i,
Che in que- ste brac- cia, che in que- ste brac- cia A- mor vi
Che in que- ste brac- cia, che in que- ste brac- cia,

78
Vn. 1
Vn. 2
A
strin- ga ma- i, Che in que- ste brac- cia, che in que- ste brac- cia A- mor
B
che in que- ste brac- cia, che in que- ste brac- cia A- mor
B.c.
82
vi strin- ga ma- i,
vi strin- ga ma- i, Che mai, mai, mai v'ab- bia a go- der den-
87
Che mai, mai, mai v'ab- bia a go- der, mai,
- tro al mio se- no, Que- st'e pro- prio un cer- car quan- d'ar- de 'l cie- lo Su l'a- re- ne del mar le bri- ne e 'l
91
mai, Que- st'e pro- prio un cer- car quan- d'ar- de 'l cie- lo Su l'a- re- ne del mar le bri- ne e 'l ge-
ge- lo. Che mai, mai, mai, mai,

-lo, Quest'e proprio un cercar quand'arde 'l cielo Su l'arene del mar le brine e 'l gelo

mai v'abbia a goder, mai, mai, dentro al mio seno,

-lo, Quest'e proprio un cercar quand'arde 'l cielo Su l'arene del

Quest'e proprio un cercar quand'arde 'l cielo Su l'a-

mar, su l'arene del mar le brine 'l gelo.

-rene del mar, su l'arene del mar le brine e 'l gelo.

9. Or che Giovanni

Or che Giovanni entr'al deserto esclama E tutti chiama: "Contriti, Fuggite, Lasciate Le colpe

passate, E fate penitenza, egri mortali, Che son vicino omai, che son vicino omai gli eterni mali, gli eterni mali.

"Fuggite i prati, Lasciate i fiori Che sono aguati De traditori. Non violette, Non fresche herbette

"Fuggite i prati, Lasciate i fiori Che sono aguati De traditori. Non violette, Non

"Fuggite i prati, Lasciate i fiori Che sono aguati De traditori.

e prenda con ogni affetto, Ogni desio vedere Dio."

prenda con ogni affetto, Ogni desio vedere Dio."

prenda con ogni affetto, Ogni desio vedere Dio."

Sinfonia seconda

"Ahi, che bramo e desio, desio Vedetti, o Dio;

Ma, ma i miei peccati Han fatto così gran macchia al core Che mirar non ti può, dolce Signore, dolce Signore."

"Versa da gl'occhi Un fonte acciocchè giunto al core Cavi la macchia del passato errore. Così mesta e pentita un dì potrai Gl'occhi fissar, gl'occhi fissar nei miei celesti rai."

127
C
T
B
B.c.
"Fug- gi- te i pra- ti, La- scia- te i fio- ri Che so- no a- gua- ti De
"Fug- gi- te i pra- ti, La- scia- te i fio- ri
"Fug- gi- te i pra- ti, La- scia- te i fio- ri
134
tra- di- to- ri, Non vi- o- let- te, Non fre- sche her- bet- te
Che so- no a- gua- ti De tra- di- to- ri, Non vi- o- let- te, Non
Che so- no a- gua- ti De tra- di- to- ri,
♯[5] 6 ♯ ♮
141
Che son fol- li- e, Che son paz-
fre- sche her- bet- te Che son fol- li- e,
Non vi- o- let- te, Non fre- sche her- bet- te Che son fol- li- e,
♮ 6

-zi- e. Al- ti pen- sie- ri, Ce- le- sti_im- pe- ri, E- ter- ne

Che son paz- zi- e. Al- ti pen- sie- ri, Ce-

Al- ti pen- sie- ri, Ce- le- sti_im-

vi- te Im- pre- se gran- di Il vo- stro pet- to_Ab- brac- ci,

-le- sti_im- pe- ri, Il vo- stro pet- to_Ab- brac- ci, e

-pe- ri, Im- pre- se gran- di Il vo- stro pet- to_Ab- brac- ci, e

e pren- da con o- gni_af- fet- to, O- gni de- si- o ve- de- re Di- o."

pren- da con o- gni_af- fet- to, O- gni de- si- o ve- de- re Di- o."

pren- da con o- gni_af- fet- to, O- gni de- si- o ve- de- re Di- o."

10. Già brutto non son io

"Già brut- to non son io se l'on- da che- ta Mo- stra- mi_il ver del- la mia ver_i- ma- go, Che mi deg- gia fug- gir, che mi

"Che mi deg- gia fug- gir, che mi deg- gia fug- gir, deg- gia fug- gir, mi deg- gia fug- gir, mi deg- gia fug- gir

"qual ti- gre_o dra- go, Che mi

20
che mi deg- gia fug- gir, fug- gir, che mi deg- gia fug-
qual ti- gre o dra- go, Che mi deg- gia fug- gir, che mi
deg- gia fug- gir, che mi deg- gia fug- gir qual ti- gre o
27
-gir qual ti- gre o dra- go, Co-
deg- gia fug- gir qual ti- gre o dra-
dra- go, Che mi deg- gia fug- gir, che mi deg- gia fug- gir,
33
-lei ch'è del mio ben prin- ci- pio, prin- ci- pi- o e
-go, Co- lei ch'è del mio ben prin- ci- pi- o e
Co- lei ch'è del mio ben prin- ci- pio e

Ritornello primo

me- tà.

"La fronte ho crespa, sì, ma però lieta; Di fiamma ho 'l volto ancor, ma puro e vago, Tal ch'arsi il cor ne 'l tuo siringa impiago,

79

im- pia- go, Di lei nel pri- mo ciel, nel pri- mo

Di lei nel pri- mo

85

ciel va- rio pia- ne- ta.

ciel va- rio pia- ne- ta.

91 Ritornello secondo

Vn. 1

Vn. 2

B.c.

98

106

B: "Dun- que con- vien ch'in ac- qua io mi di- stem- pre

B.c.

Mentre tutto nel foco ardo e sfavillo Ne tu l'empio rigor, ne tu l'empio rigor, Ninfa, ne tu l'empio rigor, Ninfa, ne tu l'empio rigor, ne tu l'empio rigor, Ninfa, con- tem- pre."

Ritornello primo di sopra

Vn. 1
Vn. 2
B.c.

Finale a 5

T1: "Sì, sì," disse Pane, e bel l'a- ma- ta u- dil- lo.

T2: "Sì, sì, sì," disse Pane, e bel l'a- ma- ta u- dil- lo.

B: "Sì, sì," disse Pane, e bel l'a- ma- ta u- dil- lo.

Non la vid- d'ei, che, fa- vel- lan- do, che, fa- vel- lan- do, che, fa- vel- lan- do sem-

74

*See critical notes.

11. Or so come da sè

16
- ra, guer- - ra, guer- ra e tre- gua,
guer- ra, guer- ra e tre- gua,
guer- ra, guer- ra e tre- gua, E co-
21
E co- prir suo do- lor, e co- prir suo do-
E co- prir suo do- lor quan-
-prir suo do- lor quan- d'al- tri il pun-
6 6 6 6
27
-lor quan- d'al- tri il pun- ge, E co-
-d'al- tri il pun- ge, E co- prir suo do- lor, suo do-
-ge, E co- prir suo do- lor, suo do- lor quan- d'al- tri il

33
-prir suo do- lor, suo do- lor quan- d'al- tri il pun- ge.
-lor quan- d'al- tri, e co- prir suo do- lor quan- d'al- - tri il pun- ge.
pun- - - - - - ge.
6 7 6 7 4 9
40
Ritornello
Vn. 1
Vn. 2
B.c.
47
53

60
A
T
B.c.
Io so co-me in un pun- to si di-
Io so co-me in un pun- to si di- le- gua
♮ ♭
65
-le- gua E poi si spar- - ge per le ve-ne il san- gue, E poi si
E poi si spar- - ge per le ve- ne il san-
♮ ♭
69
spar- ge per le ve- ne il san- gue, E poi si spar- ge per le
-gue, E poi si spar- ge per le ve- ne il san- gue,
72
ve- ne il san- gue Se pa- u- ra o ver- go- gna av- vien ch'il se-
il san- gue Se pa- u- ra o ver- go- gna av- vien ch'il
7 [♯]6 ♯ 6 5 6 5

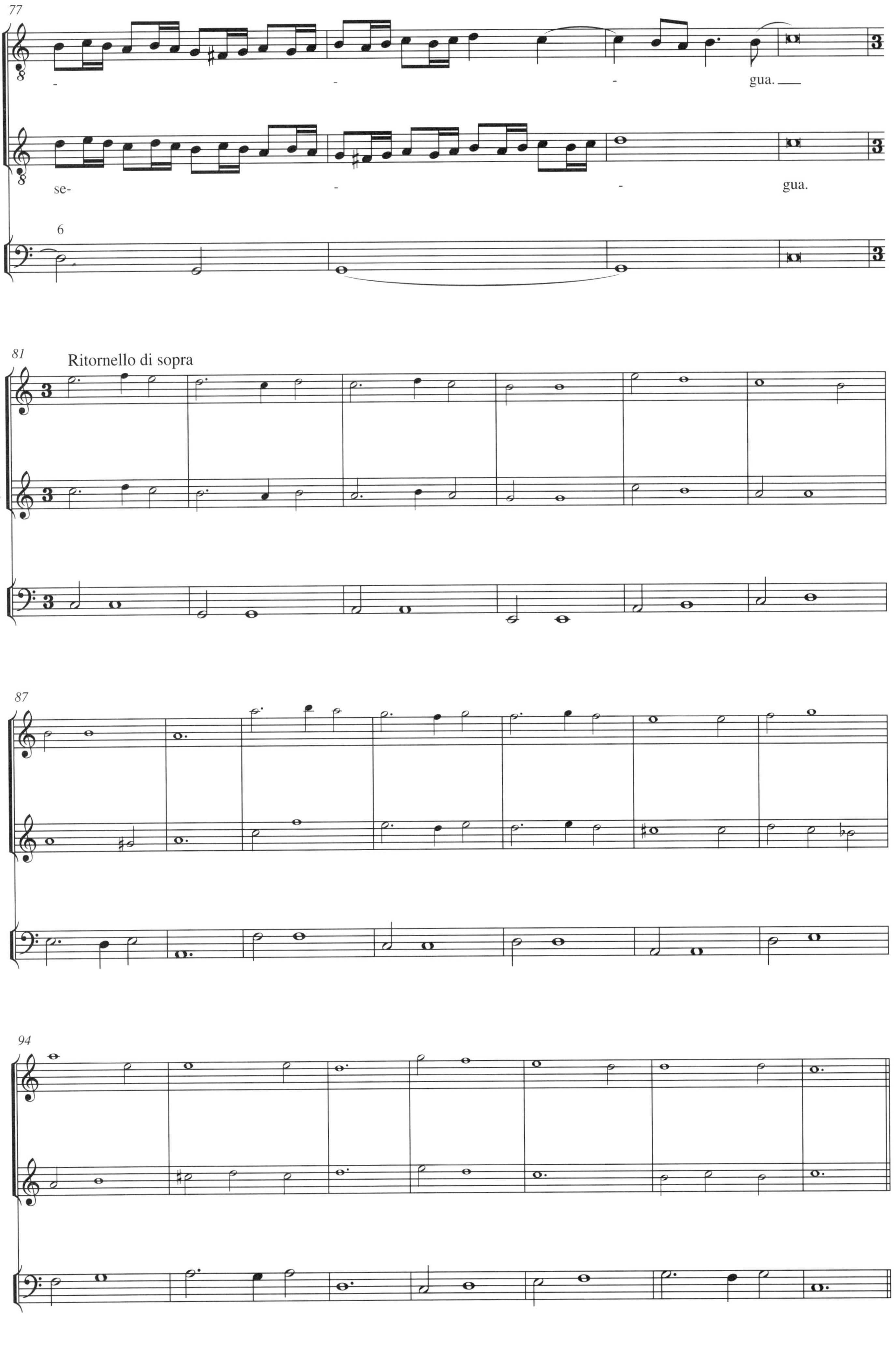
77
gua.
se-
gua.
6
81
Ritornello di sopra
Vn. 1
Vn. 2
B.c.
87
94

81

126
si
vo- - - glie e dor- me,
-me,
130
vo- - - glie e dor- me,
si
134
si vo- - glie, si vo- - glie, si
vo- glie, si vo- glie, si vo-
si vo- - glie, si vo- glie, si vo-
138
vo- glie, si vo- - glie e dor- me,
- glie, si vo- - glie e dor- - me,
- glie, si vo- - glie e dor- me,
6 ♮ 6 7 6 ♯

83

12. Su l'ali del tempo

12
-pri- le, Pur- trop- po di- scer- no Cor- re- re, cor- re- re, cor- re- re‿al ver-
gl'an- ni l'A- pri- le, Pur- trop- po di- scer- no Cor- re- re, cor- re- re, cor- re-re‿al ver-
gl'an- ni l'A- pri- le, Pur- trop- po di- scer- no Cor- re- re, cor- re- re, cor- re-re‿al ver-
6
16
-no, Ne in- die- tro ri- tor- no fa, Ne in- die- tro ri- tor- no fa, Ne in-
-no, Ne in- die- tro ri- tor- no fa, Ne in- die- tro ri- tor- no
-no, Ne in- die- tro ri- tor- no fa, Ne in- die- tro ri- tor- no fa, Ne in-
6
6
20
-die- tro ri- tor- no fa. Su l'a- li del tem- po s'en fug- ge l'e- tà. Eu-
fa, ri- tor- no fa. Su l'a- li del tem- po s'en fug- ge l'e- tà.
-die- tro ri- tor- no fa. Su l'a- li del tem- po s'en fug- ge l'e- tà.
6 6
6
1.

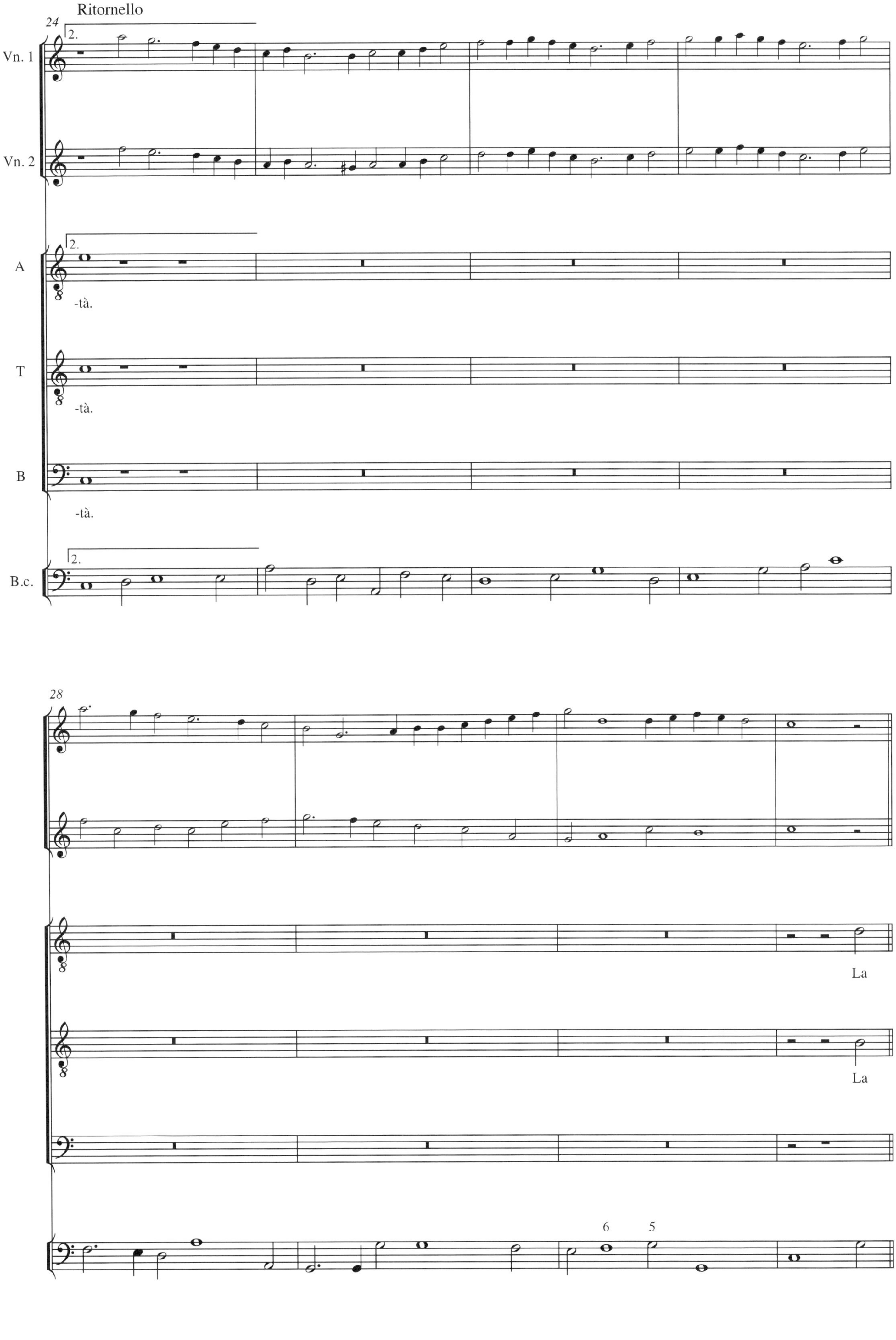
Ritornello
24
2.
Vn. 1
Vn. 2
A
-tà.
T
-tà.
B
-tà.
B.c.
28
La
La
6
5

32
A
T
B
B.c.
ro- sa, non col- ta Fio- ren- do, lan- gue, Fio- ren- do, fio- ren- do, lan-
ro- sa, non col- ta Fio- ren- do, lan- gue, Fio- ren- do, fio- ren- do, lan-
E 'l na- ti- vo co- lor sma-
35
-gue, Fio- ren- do, fio- ren- do, lan- gue E 'l na- ti- vo co- lor sma-
-gue, Fio- ren- do, fio- ren- do, lan- gue E 'l na- ti- vo co- lor sma-
-ri, E 'l na- ti- vo co- lor sma- ri, E 'l na- ti- vo co- lor sma-
38
1.
2.
-ri; La -ri; Ciò ch'al- tri si per- de Mai più si rin- ver- de; T'in- vi- ta- no
-ri; La -ri; Ciò ch'al- tri si per- de Mai più si rin- ver- de; T'in-
-ri; -ri; Ciò ch'al- tri si per- de Mai più si rin- ver- de; T'in-

43
l'o- re, Nun- zie d'a- mo- re, Nun- zie d'a- mo-
-vi- ta- no l'o- re, Nun- zie d'a- mo- re, Nun- zie d'a- mo-
-vi- ta- no l'o- re, Nun- zie d'a- mo- re, Nun- zie d'a- mo-
46
-re, A gra- dir la tua bel- tà, A gra- dir, a gra- dir la tua bel- tà, A gra-
-re, A gra- dir la tua bel- tà, A gra- dir, a gra-
-re, A gra- dir la tua bel- tà, A gra- dir, a gra- dir la tua bel-
6
49
-dir, a gra- dir la tua bel- tà. Su l'a- li del
-dir la tua bel- tà, A gra- dir la tua bel- tà. Su l'a- li del
-tà, A gra- dir la tua bel- tà, la tua bel- tà. Su l'a- li del
6 6 6 6

Ritornello

tem- po s'en fug- ge l'e- tà. Ciò -tà.

Quel vol- to, che pia- que Gran tem- po, s'o- diò, che

Se co-

64
A
pia- que Gran tem- po, s'o- diò, che pia- que Gran tem- po, s'o- diò Se co-
T
pia- que Gran tem- po, s'o- diò, che pia- que Gran tem- po, s'o- diò Se co-
B
-lor o can- dor mu- tò, Se co- lor o can- dor mu- tò, Se co-
B.c.
67
-lor o can- dor mu- tò. Quel -tò. Il tem- po, bi- fol- co, Col- ti- va quel
-lor o can- dor mu- tò. Quel -tò. Il tem- po, bi- fol- co, Col-
-lor o can- dor mu- tò. -tò. Il tem- po, bi- fol- co, Col-
72
sol- co Cui for- ma il sem- bian- te, for- ma il sem- bian- te Di vec-
-ti- va quel sol- co Cui for- ma il sem- bian- te, for- ma il sem- bian- te Di
-ti- va quel sol- co Cui for- ma il sem- bian- te, for- ma il sem- bian- te Di

-chio, di vec-chio a-man- te Che non tro- va in cor pie- tà, Che non tro- va, non

vec- chio a- man- te Che non tro- va in cor pie-

vec- chio, di vec-chio a-man- te Che non tro- va in cor pie- tà, Che non

tro- va in cor pie- tà, Che non tro- va, che non tro- va in cor pie-

-tà, Che non tro- va, non tro- va in cor pie- tà, Che non tro- va in cor pie-

tro- va, non tro- va in cor pie- tà, Che non tro- va in cor pie- tà, in cor pie-

Ritornello

-tà. Su l'a- li del tem- po s'en fug- ge l'e- tà. Il -tà.

-tà. Su l'a- li del tem- po s'en fug- ge l'e- tà. -tà.

-tà. Su l'a- li del tem- po s'en fug- ge l'e- tà. -tà.

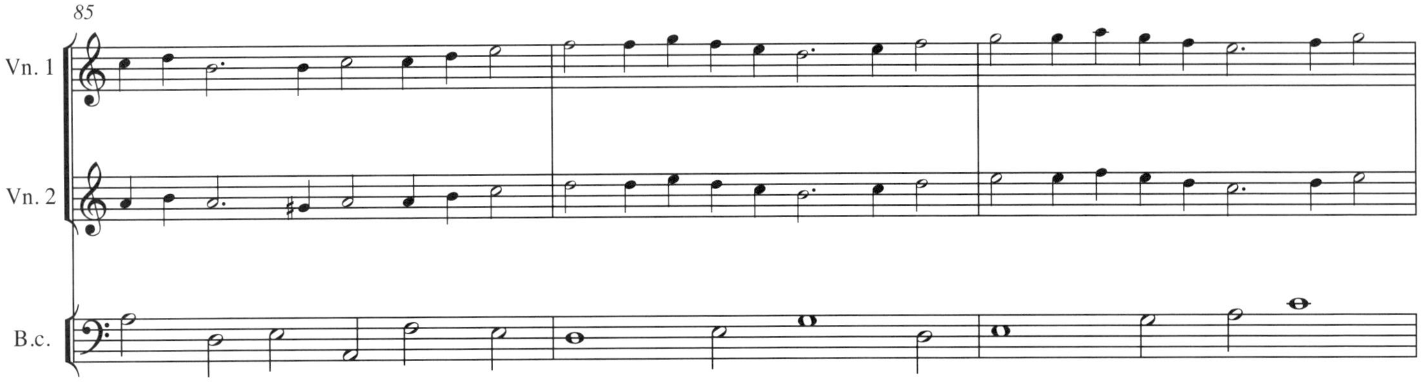
85
Vn. 1
Vn. 2
B.c.

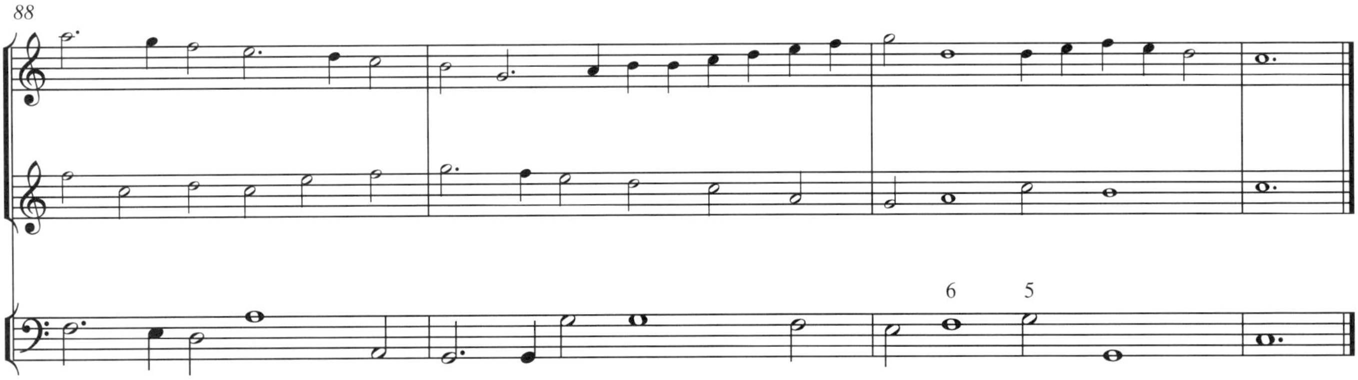
88
6
5

13. Spars'ho in pianto

*This part is optional.

15
1.
2.
21
T1
Spar-s'ho‿in pian- to‿il mio san- gue, Vez- zo- sa mia cru- del, L'al-
T2
Spar-s'ho‿in pian- to‿il mio san- gue, Vez- - zo- sa mia cru- del, L'al-
B.c.
28
-ma che lan- gue Pur vi- ve‿an- cor fe- del, Pur vi- ve‿an-
- ma che lan- gue Pur vi- ve‿an- cor, pur vi- ve‿an- cor, pur vi- ve‿an-
35
T1
-cor fe- del. Tal e sua fè che mai mer- cè Cer- cò del suo
T2
-cor fe- del. Tal e sua fè che mai mer- cè Cer- cò del suo
B
Tal e sua fè che mai mer- cè Cer- cò del suo lan-
B.c.

41

lan- guir, Si fi- da- va che mai pie- tà Cer- cò del suo mo- rir,

lan- guir, Si fi- da- va che mai pietà Cer- cò del suo mo- rir,

-guir, Si fi- da- va che mai pie- tà Cer- cò del suo mo- rir,

47

mai, mai pie- tà, pie- tà, pie- tà Cer- cò del suo mo- rir.

mai, mai pie- tà, pie- tà, pie- tà Cer- cò del suo mo- rir.

mai, mai pie- tà, pie- tà, pie- tà Cer- cò del suo mo- rir.

52 Ritornello di sopra

Vn. 1

Vn. 2

B.c.

58

Scio- glie la vo- ce, scio- glie la vo-ce il pian- to, il pian- to
E in- ve- ce sua, pur vuol, pur vuol Pre- gar- ti, o ___
___ bel- la, bel- la, tan- to Ch'io mi- ri, ch'io mi-ri un tan- to ___ duol, o ___
___ bel- la, bel- la, tan- to Ch'io mi- ri, ch'io mi-ri un tan- to ___ duol.

T1: Tal e sua fè che mai mer- cè Cer- cò del suo lan- guir,
T2: Tal e sua fè che mai mer- cè Cer- cò del suo lan- guir,
B: Tal e sua fè che mai mer- cè Cer- cò del suo lan - guir,

T1: Si fi- da- va che mai pie- tà Cer- cò del suo mo- rir,
T2: Si fi- da- va che mai pie- tà Cer- cò del suo mo- rir,
B: Si fi- da- va che mai pie- tà Cer- cò del suo mo - rir,

T1: mai, mai pie- tà, pie- tà, pie- tà Cer- cò del suo mo- rir.
T2: mai, mai pie- tà, pie- tà, pie- tà Cer- cò del suo mo- rir.
B: mai, mai pie- tà, pie- tà, pie- tà Cer- cò del suo mo- rir.

Dal pal- li- do sem- bian- te Po- tes- si, ahi, ahi, po- tes- si ben mi- rar

S'io fos- si fi- do a- man- te Quan- t'a- spro, quan- t'a- spro, quan- t'a- spro e 'l mio pe- nar, Quan- t'a- spro e 'l mio pe- nar.

T1: Tal e sua fè che mai mer- cè Cer- cò del suo lan- guir,
T2: Tal e sua fè che mai mer- cè Cer- cò del suo lan- guir,
B: Tal e sua fè che mai mer- cè Cer- cò del suo lan- guir,
B.c.

Si fi- da- va che mai pie- tà Cer- cò del suo mo- rir,
Si fi- da- va che mai pie- tà Cer- cò del suo mo- rir,
Si fi- da- va che mai pie- tà Cer- cò del suo mo- rir,

mai, mai pie- tà, pie- tà, pie- tà Cer- cò del suo mo- rir.

mai, mai pie- tà, pie- tà, pie- tà Cer- cò del suo mo- rir.

mai, mai pie- tà, pie- tà, pie- tà Cer- cò del suo mo- rir.

Ritornello di sopra

168
1.
2.
174
T1
Gran pe- na e a cor spi- ran- te Vo- ce im- pe-
T2
Gran pe- na e a cor spi- ran- te Vo- - ce im- pe-
B.c.
179
-di- ta al dir; Se 'l mio pur ta- que i- nan- te
-di- ta al dir; Se 'l mio pur ta- que i- - nan- te Non ta- que-
184
Non ta- que- rà i so- spir, Non ta- que- rà i so- spir.
-rà, non ta- que- rà, non ta- que- rà i so- spir.

T1 (mm. 190–): Tal e sua fè che mai mer- cè Cer- cò del suo lan- guir,

T2: Tal e sua fè che mai mer- cè Cer- cò del suo lan- guir,

B: Tal e sua fè che mai mer- cè Cer- cò del suo lan- guir,

B.c.

(m. 195)

T1: Si fi- da- va che mai pie- tà Cer- cò del suo mo- rir,

T2: Si fi- da- va che mai pie- tà Cer- cò del suo mo- rir,

B: Si fi- da- va che mai pie- tà Cer- cò del suo mo- rir,

(m. 200)

T1: mai, mai pie- tà, pie- tà, pie- tà Cer- cò del suo mo- rir.

T2: mai, mai pie- tà, pie- tà, pie- tà Cer- cò del suo mo- rir.

B: mai, mai pie- tà, pie- tà, pie- tà Cer- cò del suo mo- rir.

14. Aure placide e volanti

-ti, Messagere del l'Aurora, Che di rose e d'amaranti Ingemmate il crin a Flora, Chi di voi, chi di voi gli eccelsi onori Canterà, canterà, canterà de la mia Clori, Chi di voi, chi di voi gli eccelsi onori Canterà, canterà, canterà de la mia Clori?

Ritornello di sopra

40
Vn. 1
Vn. 2
B.c.
44
48
Vn. 1
Vn. 2
T
Zef- fi- ret- ti che scuo-
B.c.
52
T
-te- te Va- ghi fior di pa- ra- di- so, Poi ch'in ciel por- ta- to ha-
B.c.
56
-ve- te Il va- lor di quel bel vi- so, Chi di-

60
-rà, chi di- rà s'io tac- cio e mo- ro Per co- lei, per co- lei che
64
tan- to a- - do- ro, Chi di- rà, chi di- rà s'io tac-
68
- cio e mo- ro Per co- lei, per co- lei che tan- - to a- do-
72
Ritornello di sopra
Vn. 1
Vn. 2
T
-ro?
B.c.
76
Vn. 1
Vn. 2
B.c.
80

Vn. 1
Vn. 2
C
B.c.
S'io m'ap- pres- so a i lu- mi ar- den- ti Gran ti- mor la lin- gua af-
-fre- na, Gran ti- mor la lin- gua af- fre- na, A lei, dun- que, au-
-ret- te e ven- - ti, Pa- le- sa- te la mia pe- na.
Chi pro- vò, chi pro- vò d'A-mor gli stra- li Muo- ve- rà più rat- to
l'a- li, Chi pro- vò, chi pro- vò d'A-mor gli stra- li Muo- ve- rà
Ritornello di sopra
più rat- to l'a- li.

108
Vn. 1
Vn. 2
B.c.
112
116
Finale tutti
C
T
B
Un dì, voi, mos- so a pie- ta- de,
Un dì, voi, mos- so a pie- ta- de,
Un dì, voi, mos- so a pie- ta- de, A lei
120
Lun- ga- men- te, al- ta bel- ta- de,
Lun- ga- men- te, al- ta bel- ta- de,
di- ca i miei so- spi- ri
Lun- ga- men- te,

124
Lun- ga- men- te, al- ta bel- ta- de
Lun- ga- men- te, al- ta bel- ta- de
al- ta bel- ta- de Non e rea, non e rea d'as- pri mar-
128
Chi pro- vò d'A- mor gli stra- li Muo- ve- rà,
Chi pro- vò d'A- mor gli stra- li Muo- ve- rà, muo- ve-
-ti- ri. Chi pro- vò d'A- mor gli stra- li Muo- ve- rà, muo- ve-
132
muo- ve- rà, muo- ve- rà più rat- to l'a- li, Chi pro-
-rà, muo- ve- rà, muo- ve- rà più rat- to l'a- li, Chi pro-
-rà, muo- ve- rà, muo- ve- rà più rat- to l'a- li, Chi pro-

136
-vò d'A- mor gli stra- li Muo- ve- rà, muo- ve- rà,
-vò d'A- mor gli stra- li Muo- ve- rà, muo- ve- rà, muo- ve-
-vò d'A- mor gli stra- li Muo- ve- rà, muo- ve- rà, muo- ve-
140
Vn. 1
Vn. 2
C
muo- ve- rà più rat- - to l'a- - li.
T
-rà, muo- ve- rà più rat- to l'a- li.
B
-rà, muo- ve- rà più rat- to l'a- li.
B.c.

15. Per torbido mare

9
1.
2.
Per
-ro. Per -ro.
Non spe- ri mia
-ro. Per -ro. Ma giun- ger in por- to Non spe- ri mia fè, Non
13
A
fè S'in pop- pa for- tu- na Non spi- ra per me, S'in pop- pa for- -tu- na Non spi- ra per
T
fè S'in pop- pa for- tu- na Non spi- ra per me, S'in pop- pa for- -tu- na Non spi- ra per
B
spe- ri mia fè, Non spe- ri mia fè, Non
B.c.
17
Vn. 1
Vn. 2
A
me, Non spe- ri mia fè, Non spe- ri mia fè S'in pop- pa for-
T
me, Non spe- ri mia fè, Non spe- ri mia fè S'in pop- pa for-
B
spe- ri mia fè S'in pop- pa for- tu- na Non spi- ra per me, S'in
B.c.

*See the critical notes for a discussion of this ritornello.

33
Vn. 1
Vn. 2
A
T
B
B.c.
2.
Bel- lez- ze, ch'a- do- ro Con vo- glie a- mo- ro- se, Di no- bil te- so- ro Son
Bel- lez- ze, ch'a- do- ro Con vo- glie a- mo- ro- se, Di no- bil te- so- ro Son
Bel- lez- ze, ch'a- do- ro Con vo- glie a- mo- ro- se, Di no- bil te- so- ro Son
6
37
mer- ci pom- po- se, Son mer- ci, son mer- ci, son mer- ci pom- po- se.
mer- ci pom- po- se, Son mer- ci, son mer- ci, son mer- ci, son mer- ci pom- po-
mer- ci pom- po- se, Son mer- ci, son mer- ci, son mer- ci, son mer- ci pom- po-

41
1.
2.
Bel- Sospiri co-
-se. Bel- -se. Sospiri co-
-se. Bel- -se. Del arso mio core Sospiri concenti, So-
45
A
-centi Per l'onda d'amore Son placidi venti, Per l'onda d'amore Son placidi
T
-centi Per l'onda d'amore Son placidi venti, Per l'onda d'amore Son placidi
B
-spiri concenti, Sospiri concenti, So-
B.c.
49
Vn. 1
Vn. 2
A
venti, Sospiri concenti, Sospiri concenti Per l'onda d'a-
T
venti, Sospiri concenti, Sospiri concenti Per l'onda d'a-
B
-spiri concenti Per l'onda d'amore Son placidi venti, Per
B.c.

*See critical notes.

16. Io, che piansi

*The canto secondo part can also be sung by a tenor an octave lower, or both canto parts can be sung by tenors.

118

*For suggested emendation of mm. 15–16 see critical notes.

38
-vo il tuo bu- giar- do co- re Qual fo- glia al ven- -
-giar- do co- re Qual fo-glia al ven- to
-re, Or veg- gio e pro- vo il tuo bu- giar- do co- re Qual fo- glia al ven-

42
-to in- sta- bil e va- gan- te, Qual fo- glia al ven-
in- sta- bil e va- gan- te, in- sta- bil e va- gan-
-to in- sta- bil e va- gan- te,

46
-to in- sta- bil e va- gan- te, Tu, lon-
-te, in- sta- bil e va- gan- te, Tu, lon- ta- no da
Qual fo- glia al ven- to Tu, lon- ta- no da me, tor-
50
-ta- no da me, tor- ci le pian- te, tor- ci le pian-
me, tor- ci le pian- te, tor- - ci le pian- -
- ci le pian- te, tor- ci le pian- te, tor- ci le pian-

55
-te Do- v'hai lac- ci di fè, do- v'hai lac- ci di fè frut-
-te Do- v'hai lac- ci di fè, do- v'hai lac- ci di fè frut-
-te Do- v'hai lac- ci di fè, do- v'hai lac- ci di fè frut-
61
Ritornello di sopra
- to d'a- mo- re.
-to d'a- mo- re.
- to d'a- mo- re.
66
Vn. 1
Vn. 2
B.c.

C1: Tor- na, deh, tor- na e non vo- ler che si- a Pre- mio di fe- de- lis- si- ma con- sor- te Il tra- di- men- to tuo, la pe- na mi- a.

C2: Che se ne l'in- co-

B: Che se ne l'in- co- stan- z'an- cor se

Finale tutti

91
Che se ne l'in- co- stan- z'an- cor se for- te
-stan- z'an- cor se for- te, Che se ne l'in- co-
for- te, Che se ne l'in- co- stan- z'an- cor se for-
96
Sap- pi ch'o- ve pie- tà
-stan- z'an- cor se for- te Sap- pi ch'o- ve pie- tà
-te, Che se ne l'in- co- stan- z'an- cor se for- te Sap- pi ch'o- ve pie-

100
non mi ti di- a, non mi ti di- a,
non mi ti di- a, Sap- pi ch'o- ve pie-
-tà non mi ti di- a,
104
non mi ti di- a
-tà non mi ti di- a
Sap- pi ch'o- ve pie- tà non mi ti di- a

Darà morte a due vite una sol morte, Darà morte a due vite una sol morte.

17. Una fanciulla

Canto: U- na fan-ciul- la m'ha ru- ba- to il cor. M'ha pri- vo di li- ber- tà Que- sta cru- da d'A- mor. U- na fan-ciul- la m'ha ru- ba- to il cor. Son pre- so,

Tenore: U- na fan-ciul- la m'ha ru- ba- to il cor. Son

Basso: U- na fan-ciul- la m'ha ru- ba- to il cor. Son

*See the critical notes on the possibility of beginning with the ritornello.

8
C
son le- ga- to, io mo- ro. E pur que- sta cru-
T
pre- so, son le- ga- to, io mo- - ro. E pur que- sta cru-
B
pre- so, son le- ga- to, io mo- ro. E pur que- sta cru-
B.c.
12
-del non vol u- dir I miei so-spir, i miei do-lor.
-del non vol u- dir I miei so- spir, i miei do- lor. U- na fan-ciul- la
-del non vol u- dir I miei so- spir, i miei do- lor.
16
Ritornello
Vn. 1
Vn. 2
C
U- na fan- ciul- la m'ha ru- ba- to il cor.
T
m'ha ru- ba- to il cor, U- na fan- ciul- la m'ha ru- ba- to il cor.
B
U- na fan- ciul- la m'ha ru- ba- to il cor.
B.c.

Vn. 1
Vn. 2
B.c.
C
T
B
U- na fan- ciul- la m'ha fe- ri- to il sen. E non tro- vo, ohi- mè, pie- tà Quan- to
più ven- go men. U- na fan- ciul- la m'ha fe- ri- to il sen. Son pun- to,
son pia- ga- to, io spi- ro. E pur la cru- da o-
U- na fan- ciul- la m'ha fe- ri- to il sen. Son
pun- to, son pia- ga- to, io spi- - ro. E pur la cru- da o-
U- na fan- ciul- la m'ha fe- ri- to il sen. Son
pun- to, son pia- ga- to, io spi- ro. E pur la cru- da o-

-gn'or pri- va di fè, Ne- ga mer- cè, mi dà ve- len.

-gn'or pri- va di fè, Ne- ga mer- cè, mi dà ve- len. U- na fan-ciul- la

-gn'or pri- va di fè, Ne- ga mer- cè, mi dà ve- len.

Ritornello

U- na fan-ciul- la m'ha fe- ri- to il sen,

m'ha fe- ri- to il sen, U- na fan-ciul- la m'ha fe- ri- to il sen,

U- na fan-ciul- la m'ha fe- ri- to il sen,

Finale tutti

m'ha fe-ri- to, m'ha fe-ri- to, m'ha fe-ri- to il sen, m'ha fe-ri- to, m'ha fe-ri- to, m'ha fe-ri- to il sen.

18. Addio begl'occhi

9
ad- dio be- gl'oc- chi, be- gl'oc- chi, ad- di- o,
ad- dio be- gl'oc- chi, be- gl'oc- chi, ad-
12
ad- dio be- gl'oc- chi, ad- di- o, ad - dio be-
ad- di- o, ad- di- o, ad- di- o,
-di- o,
Ad- di- o, ad- di- o, ad- di- o, ad- dio be- gl'oc- chi, be-

16
Vn. 1
Vn. 2
C1
ad- di- o, ad- dio stel-
C2
-gl'oc- chi, ad- di- o,
A
ad- di- o, ad- dio stel- le se- re- ne, Ca- gion
T
ad- di- o,
B
-gl'oc- chi, ad- di- o, ad- di- o, ad- dio stel- le se- re- ne, Ca- gion,
B.c.
20
-le se- re- ne, Ca- gion, ad- dio, stel- le se- re- ne, ca- gion del- le mie
ad- dio stel- le se- re- ne, Ca- gion,
ad- dio stel- le se- re- ne, Ca- gion, ca- gion, ca- gion del- le mie
ad- dio stel- le se- re- ne, ca- gion, ca- gion del- le mie
5 [♯]4 6

24
pe- - ne, ad- dio stel- le se- re- ne, Ca-gion, ca- gion
del- le mie pe- - ne,
pe- ne,
ad- dio stel-
pe- ne,
ad- dio stel- le se- re- ne, Ca-gion, ca-
4 ♭6 4 ♯
29
del- le mie pe- - ne,
del- le mie pe- - ne,
del- le mie pe- - ne,
-le se- re- ne, Ca- gion del- le mie pe- ne,
-gion, ca- gion, ca- gion del- le mie pe- ne,
[6] [♭]6 4 ♮

Poi- chè quan- - do vi mi- ro Ver- so la- gri- me o gn'o- ra,
Poi- chè quan- - do vi mi- ro,
Poi- chè quan- - do vi mi- ro
Poi- chè quan- - do vi mi- ro Ver- so
Poi- chè quan- - do vi mi- ro,

ver- so la- gri- me o gn'o- ra, o- gn'or, o- gn'or, o-
Ver- so la- gri- me o gn'o- ra, o- gn'or, o- gn'or,
la- gri- me o gn'o- ra, ver- so la- gri- me o gn'o- ra, o- gn'or, o- gn'or

42
-gn'or so- spi- ro, Poi- chè quan- - do vi mi- ro
Poi- chè quan- - do vi mi- ro Ver- so
Poi- chè quan- - do vi mi- ro
so- spi- ro, Poi- chè quan- - do vi mi- ro
Poi- chè quan- - do vi mi- ro
♯4
5

46
C1
C2
la- gri- me o- gn'o- ra, ver- so la- gri- me o- gn'o- ra, o-
A
T
Ver- so la- gri- me o- gn'o- ra, ver- so la- gri- me o- gn'o- ra,
B
Ver- so la- gri- me o- gn'o- ra, ver- so la- gri- me o- gn'o- ra,
6
6
B.c.

50
-gn'or, o- gn'or, o- gn'or so- spi- ro, o- gn'or, o- gn'or, o- gn'or so- spi-
o- gn'or, o- gn'or, o- gn'or so- spi-
o- gn'or, o- gn'or so- spi- ro.
o- gn'or, o- gn'or so- spi- ro.
6 ♯4 ♮ ♯
54
-ro, o- gn'or, o- gn'or, o- gn'or so- spi- ro, so- spi-
-ro, o- gn'or, o- gn'or so- spi- ro, so- spi-

58
Vo- glio da voi par- ti- re Ch'io non pos- so
-ro. Vo- glio da voi par- ti- re Ch'io non pos- so
-ro. Vo- glio da voi par- ti- re
Vo- glio da voi par- ti- re
Vo- glio da voi par- ti- re Ch'io non pos-
♯ ♯ [♯]6 6
62
mi- rar- vi e non mo- - ri- re,
mi- rar- vi e non mo- - ri- re,
Ch'io non pos- so mi-
Ch'io non pos- so mi-
- so mi- rar- vi e non mo- ri- re,

67
Ch'io non pos- so mi- rar- vi e non
-rar- vi e non mo- ri- re, non
-rar- vi e non mo- ri- re,
Ch'io non pos- so mi-
72
Vn. 1
Vn. 2
C1
mo- ri- re,
C2
Ch'io non pos- so mi- rar- vi e non
A
mo- ri- - re,
T
B
-rar- vi e non mo- ri- re,
4 ♯3
B.c.

77
mo- ri- re, non pos- so mi- rar- vi‿e non
non pos- so mi- rar- vi,

82
non pos- so mo- ri- re, non pos- so, non pos- so mi-
mo- ri- re, non pos- so, non pos- so mi-
non pos- so mo- ri- re,
non pos- so,
non pos- so,

[sheet music]

94
non pos- so, non pos- so mi- rar- vi
-rar- vi,
non pos- so, non pos- so mi- rar- vi,
non pos- so, non pos- so mi- rar- vi
e
non mo- ri-
-rar- vi,
5
♮
[♯]6
4
98
e
non mo- ri- - re,
non pos- so, non pos- so mi- rar- vi,
- re,
non pos- so, non pos- so mi-
non pos- so, non pos- so mi- rar- vi,
[♯]3
5
6

102
non pos- so, non pos- so mi-
non pos- so, non pos- so mi- rar- vi,
-rar- vi e non mo- ri- - re,
non pos-so, non pos-so mi- rar- vi e
5 6 ♮ 5
106
Vn. 1
Vn. 2
C1
C2
-rar- vi e non mo- ri- re,
non pos- so, non pos- so mi-
A
T
e non mo- ri- re,
B
non mo- ri- - re,
B.c.
6 ♭

110
non pos- so, non pos- so mi-rar- vi
-rar- vi e non mo- ri- re,
non pos- so, non pos- so mi- rar- vi e non mo-
e non mo- ri- re, e
6 5 4 [♯]
114
e non mo- ri- - re.
e non mo- ri- - re.
-ri- re, mo- ri- - re.
non mo- ri- re, e non mo- - ri- re.
e non mo- ri- - - re.
[♯]6 4 ♯

Critical Report

Source

The sole surviving copy of the print is in Wrocław, Universytet Wrocławski, Biblioteka Uniwersytecka (PL-WRu). The title page (see plate 1) reads:

COMPOSITIONI VARIE | PER MUSICA DI CAMERA | A Due, Tre, Quattro, Cinque, Voci, e parte con due Violini | DEDICATE | All'Illustrissimo, & Reverendissimo Signor il Signor | D. VALERIANO SCAGLIA | ABBATE GENERALE DELL'ORDINE OLIVETANO | DA BIAGIO MARINI | Gentil'huomo, & Cavagliere del Sereniss. Palatino di Noiburg. | OPERA DECIMA TERZA. | IN VENETIA, | Apresso Alessandro Vincenti. MDCXXXXI.

According to Emil Bohn's catalogue of printed music in the library, it originally comprised six partbooks.[1] Two partbooks, containing the first and second violin parts, respectively, plus, presumably, the canto secondo and alto parts for the final piece, "Addio begl'occhi," were apparently destroyed during the bombardment of the library in 1945. Four partbooks exist today: "Canto ò Tenore, overo Alto" (abbreviated as C in the critical notes below), "Tenore" (T), "Basso" (B), and "Basso continuo" (B.c.). Bohn gives no measurements for the partbooks but simply describes them as "quarto." On a recent trip to Wrocław I found the size of each of the surviving partbooks to be roughly 8 ¾" high by 6 ¼" wide. This size is adequate for singers to hold in their hands but would be awkward for violinists to play comfortably from. Performance problems would have been compounded for the final piece as the violinist playing the violino primo part might have had to share a partbook with the person singing the canto secondo part, and similarly for the individuals performing the violino secondo and alto parts.

Editorial Procedures

The sung texts as printed in the source present numerous problems.[2] Spelling is inconsistent, even within the same piece, while wording can differ between partbooks. In this edition non-substantive divergences in the texts between partbooks have been tacitly regularized, while more substantive differences are reported in the critical notes. Spelling has generally been modernized and capitalization has been reserved for the beginnings of lines and for proper names. Punctuation has been added as it is generally lacking in the partbooks. Text repetitions indicated in the partbooks by *ii* have been written out in the edition, and elisions are added as needed in the underlay. In "Or che Giovanni" and "Già brutto non son io," quotation marks have been added as needed to mark the beginning of a new stanza or a change in speaker. The texts in this edition are based on the settings found in the partbooks, even in cases of texts drawn from known poetic sources. Where possible texts have been compared with modern editions or other musical settings.

With the exception of final *longae* (which are set as breves), the original note values have been retained. Although occasionally inconsistent in the source, the original meter signatures have also been retained unless indicated otherwise in the critical notes. Modern barring has been adopted; double-thin barlines are added to articulate sectional divisions in the pieces.[3] First and second endings have been added as necessary. Terms such as "Sinfonia," "Ritornello," and "Finale" that are found in the partbooks (only appearing in nos. 6 through 18) are set at the top of the score in the edition. The slurs of the partbooks have been retained and ties have been added as needed to accommodate the editorial barring; dashed slurs or ties indicate editorial additions. Other editorial additions are enclosed in square brackets.

Rather than just presenting the surviving basso continuo parts for those sections labeled "Sinfonia," "Ritornello," or "Finale," or other passages in pieces nos. 6 through 18 where the two violins most likely played, the editor has included reconstructed violin parts. When possible, material from the vocal parts has been used as a basis for the reconstructions. In "Che non senta per voi," for instance, the violin parts are based on the vocal parts in the triple-meter sections of that piece. The concluding sections labeled "Finale" also have cues such as "a 4," "a 5," or "tutti," suggesting that the violins played during the entire section; the editor has been conservative in this regard, however. These cues appear inconsistently in the partbooks even within a single work, but as shown in the edition, "a 4" or "a 5" appear mostly in nos. 6, 8, 10, and 11, while "tutti" appears almost exclusively in nos. 14, 15, 16, and 17. For the final piece, "Addio begl'occhi," the editor has provided reconstructions of the missing canto secondo and alto parts, again based on material in the surviving voice parts. All of the reconstructed parts are set using smaller-sized notation in the edition.

As with the other Marini prints in the Wrocław collection, there are occasional emendations entered by hand. In the case of the *Compositioni varie* most involve accidentals. They may have been made at different times, as there are different thicknesses of ink. As with the slips of paper pasted in, some of the inked-in accidentals could have been made at the printer's after the print run. It is not unreasonable to suppose that others may have been entered by the first users of the Wrocław copies, among them Daniel Sartorius who appears to have been a driving force behind the acquisition of these materials.[4] Some of the emendations may be open to question, but they have generally been included in this edition since, most likely dating from the seventeenth century, they might shed some light on performance practice during that time. They have been enclosed in parentheses in this edition and placed to the left of the note they affect; in general, they will not be mentioned in the critical notes below. All editorially added accidentals are placed in square brackets. Unless canceled, accidentals hold for the entire measure, and redundant accidentals in the source, whether printed or handwritten, which fall within a modern measure of the edition, have been removed tacitly.

Figures in the continuo part that appear to have been handwritten in the source are placed in parentheses above the note they affect. Editorial additions of figures are placed in brackets above the note they affect. The sharp and flat signs when used as figures indicate raised and lowered intervals, respectively. In accordance with modern usage, a natural sign is used as needed in place of an original sharp figure to indicate a raised interval, and in place of an original flat figure to indicate a lowered interval. With a few exceptions the editor has generally refrained from adding figures. Where appropriate, the horizontal placement of figures has been tacitly adjusted to line up with the scored-up voice parts.

Critical Notes

The abbreviations of voice parts used in the critical notes refer to the partbook in which the part is located, as follows: C = Canto ò Tenore, overo Alto; T = Tenore; B = Basso; B.c. = Basso continuo. Please note that these abbreviations do not necessarily correspond to the name of the voice part seen in the edition; for instance, for "Torna l'inverno, frigido," the canto secondo part is located in the tenor partbook (although this situation is clarified with the voice name provided in parentheses in some cases). Abbreviations for original note values (modern unreduced equivalents in parentheses) are br = breve, sbr = semibreve (whole note), min = minim (half note), smin = semiminim (quarter), cr = croma (eighth), scr = semicroma (sixteenth). Notes are numbered consecutively within a measure. Pitches are identified using the system in which c' = middle C.

1. Torna l'inverno, frigido

Mm. 6–7, C and T, melisma on "-do" extends from note 3 of m. 6 through note 1 of m. 7; a melisma on the first syllable of "Scac-cia" from note 4 of m. 6 through note 2 of next measure is less awkward.   Mm. 13, 16–17, 19, 51–52, 54, 72, 75, 105, 108–9, 111, C and T, the note values in the musical phrase that first appears in m. 13 at the line "Che d'ogni tempo nel mio petto" and is repeated in subsequent verses are inconsistent (dotted vs. even) in the source when the phrase is sung by the two voices either together or in imitation; the editor has adopted the dotted rhythm for notes 4–7 of that phrase.   M. 22, C, meter (proportional) signature is **3**.   M. 34, T, text is "perde i".   M. 63, C, notes 6–7 are cr–cr.   M. 65, C, note 8 is c".   Mm. 66–67, B.c., single figure ♯ between the two sbr As may apply to both, as shown in edition.

2. Ecco ch'io manco

M. 7, T, slur is on notes 1–2 with syllable "man-", and "-co" is in m. 8; in the edition, the slur is extended from note 2 to m. 8, note 1, with "-co" moved to coincide with the slur, so as to conform with mm. 15–16.

3. Miratemi o begl'occhi

M. 33, C, note 3, text underlay has "qual"; changed to "o" to conform with first phrase in m. 32.   Mm. 42–43, T, last two notes of m. 42 and first note of m. 43, text is "s'appresa".   M. 49, T, note 7 is c'; changed by printer to d' in source.   M. 52, T, note 1 has superfluous "de" underlay.   M. 56, T, note 7, underlay is "à".   M. 58, C, text of last four notes is "rivolgele à".   M. 62, C, note 5, ♭ may be misplaced and meant for the following note; there is no corresponding figure ♭ in the B.c., but an A-flat makes for effective text painting on "cieco abisso".   M. 64, T, note 1, text is "o".

4. Deh, come in un momento

M. 6, C (alto), notes 1 and 5, each has printed cautionary ♯ (indicating ♮); B, note 3 has printed cautionary ♯ (indicating ♮).   M. 8, B, note 2 has cautionary ♭, rather than note 1.   M. 16, B, note values are min–dotted min–smin, which are changed to conform with tenor part.   M. 28, T, note 5 has printed ♯.   Mm. 38–39, C, text underlay for note 3 of m. 38 and note 1 of m. 39 (presumably "l'alma") is blotted out in source.   M. 50, T, note 2, text is "voi", and m. 51, notes 1–3, text is "ch'in un un"; in edition, "ah" is repeated at the end of m. 50, "voi" is moved to the start of m. 51, and "ch'in" is moved to m. 51, note 2.   M. 60, B, meter (proportional) signature is **3**, rather than 3/2 as in the other partbooks; notes 2–3, printer's correction changing a–b to b–c'.

5. Qui, dove il sol

M. 14, B, note 1, second "i" of "-li i" missing in text underlay.   Mm. 69–70, T, all five notes and words of text missing in printed part; they have been handwritten at bottom right corner of page (see plate 2).   M. 74, T, note 3 has underlay "-re".   M. 87, B.c., figures 7 6 are over the G, but they belong over the A of the previous measure. M. 89, T, note 1 has printed cautionary ♯ (indicating ♮). Mm. 92–95, T, text of last note of m. 92 through second note of m. 95 is "in questo sito ameno"; changed to conform with C (alto).   M. 108, B, note 8 has printed cautionary ♯ (indicating ♮).   M. 112, C, note 6 has printed cautionary ♯ (indicating ♮).   M. 131, B.c., note 3, figures are ♯ and 6; the 6 belongs over note 4.

6. Pastorella

M. 28, B.c., notehead is smaller in source, possibly indicating later insertion made by printer.   M. 74, B.c., figure 7 is over second note in source.   M. 108, B, cue is "Dimmi Tacet" in source (instead of "Ecco almeno").   M. 119, B.c., note 2, ♭ is printed above note in source.   M. 131, B.c., dotted sbr in source, changed to sbr–min to conform with other iterations of the ritornello.   M. 154, B.c., note 1 has printed cautionary ♭.   M. 165, B, meter signature is ₵.

7. Non fuggir, vago augello

Although there are no ritornelli in the piece, it is labeled *A4*, thus indicating the use of two violins as well as the two voices. The alto part is printed in the C partbook while the tenor is in the T partbook. At m. 21 in the B.c. partbook, the cue indicating the beginning of a solo passage for the tenor is "Tenori"; this could be a misprint but could also indicate that there was more than one singer to a part.

M. 21, B.c., note 3 is d; changed by printer to e.   M. 40, T, text is missing "è" in "sereno è il ciel".   M. 56, T, note 2 may originally have had a printed ♯, which was later scratched out.   M. 77, B.c., note 3 has figure ♭, which may have been a misprint for figure 6.   M. 88, C, text underlay in source indicates "pro-" on note 1 and "-cel-" on remaining notes; note 5 has printed ♯.

8. Che non senta per voi

C, B, B.c., *Tavole* have "Ch'io non senta per voi".   M. 22, B.c., note 1, figure is ♭; replaced by 6 in edition.   Mm. 24–31, C, B, the contraction of "che il" is spelled both as "che 'l" and "ch'il"; editor has adopted the latter for consistency.   Mm. 26–33, C, B, "veleno" is consistently spelled "veneno".   Mm. 34 and 69, C, meter (proportional) signature is $\frac{4}{6}$; B, meter (proportional) signature is **3**, which is used in edition.   Mm. 89, 92, 96, 100, 101, C, B, "arde il" and "arde 'l" both used; editor has adopted the latter for consistency.   M. 98, B.c., figures are 4 9; as indicated in the edition, the measure consists of a 3–4–3 cadential suspension.

9. Or che Giovanni

M. 9, B.c., note 2 is A; changed by printer to B♭.   M. 10, B.c., note is B♭; changed by printer to A.   Mm. 35–39, B.c., beginning with note 2 of m. 35 the notes appear to have been written in—not only are the notes crowded together but the lines of the staff have been extended in handwritten ink and a fermata was written in m. 39; it is noteworthy that almost the first third of the next staff is empty.   Mm. 40, 127, C, meter (proportional) signature is **3**.   Mm. 48, 135, B.c., figures are ♯ and ♭; the latter may be a misprint for figure 6 added in edition in following measure.   M. 71, C, T, note 1, text is "-cia"; editor has adopted reading of "abbracci" as given in B and in Anerio's setting.   M. 77, B.c., indication is "Sinfonia seconda", but given that the continuo line is identical with that of the opening sinfonia, the violin parts were most likely also identical.   M. 98, C, note has cautionary ♭ (indicating ♮) handwritten in source.

10. Già brutto non son io

Mm. 1, 39, 60, 91, 106 (B), 141, 169, meter (proportional) signature is $\frac{4}{3}$.   Mm. 33–38, B, the text "colei . . . metà" was printed on thin paper strips and was pasted into the source.   M. 34, C (tenore primo), note 4, text is "cor".   M. 38, B.c. has fermata.   Mm. 78–79, T (tenore secondo), text underlay suggests "si-" under note 2 and "-rin-" under note 3 of m. 78, and "-ga_im-" under note 1 and "-pia-" under notes 2–5 of m. 79.   M. 90, B.c., note is sbr rather than dotted min.   Mm. 165–66, B, text is "e ben l'aurata".   M. 178, C, note 2 is f; changed by printer to e.   Mm. 185–86, T, ten cromas followed by semiminim in source, c'–b–c'–d'–c'–d'–b–a–b–c'–b.   M. 191, C, note is c'; changed by printer to d'.   M. 208, B.c., note 2 has ♯ and also has figure 6 over note.

11. Or so come da sè

M. 14, B, text underlay in source places "ce e" under note 2 and first syllable of "guerra" under note 3.   Mm. 33–38, B, the six-measure length of the low G on "pun-" might indicate a need for more than one singer on this part.   Mm. 76–77, B.c., figures are 5 6 5 6 5; should be reversed, as shown in edition.   M. 134, C (alto), text underlay places "-me" of "dorme" under note 1 rather than under note 3 of preceding measure (and slurred to following note) as is usually the case.   M. 139, T, note 5 has cautionary ♯ handwritten in source.   M. 146, B.c., figure 6 is over note 2.

12. Su l'ali del tempo

This work illustrates the problems one encounters when transcribing the music into modern measures. Although the basic movement is six minims, the opening "measure" is clearly indicated in the source as comprising two minims rest and a "pickup" note, making it three minims in duration. Similarly, the respective second sections of each strophe (mm. 9, 39, and 69) begin with a "pickup to downbeat" sense. The concluding note of each section is an imperfect semibreve (comprising two minims). Accordingly, measures 31 and 61, the respective concluding measures of the first and second iterations of the ritornello, comprise three rather than six minims. Measure 91, the final measure of the piece, has been transcribed as a perfect semibreve. In order to simplify the editorially added measure numbering, then, each barred measure, whether of six or three minims, is counted as a separate measure.

M. 11, T, notes 4–6, each has printed cautionary ♯ (indicating ♮).   M. 22, B.c., "violini" is printed over notes 3 and 4, most likely intended as a cue for the violins to prepare to play the ritornello; this also holds for mm. 52 and 82 (the b.c. part for all three verses is written out only once in the source).   M. 34, T, notes 2–3 are min–min. M. 62, T, notes 5–6 are dotted min–smin.   M. 68, T, note 1, text is "-tà".   M. 81, B, "piano" is printed over note 1.

13. Spars'ho in pianto

As in "Per torbido mare" below, there are issues concerning how the sections of this piece relate in terms of tempo. Movement in the ritornellos and the vocal sections in common time is by semiminim (quarter note), while the sections beginning "Spars'ho," "Tal e sua fè," and "Gran pena e a cor" move in minims (half notes). Performers must decide if the minim and semiminim remain roughly constant throughout the piece.

Mm. 39–51, 92–104, 141–53, 192–204, B, text underlay in source is "cercò del mio languir si fidava che mai pietà mostrò del suo morir."   Mm. 37, 90, 139, 190, C (tenore primo), note 2 is e′.   Mm. 44–45, C, text is "piata".   M. 129, T (tenore secondo), "asti" is printed between "[po]tessi" and "ben".   Mm. 183–84, T, text is "laquetrà".   Mm. 185–86, T, text is "taquerrà".

14. Aure placide e volanti

Mm. 13, 50, 84, 117, B.c., notes 1–2 are dotted min–smin.   M. 15, B.c., notes are min–min (lack dots).   M. 22, B, notes 1–2, text is "fora".   M. 31, B, note 2, ♭ may have been printed.   M. 38, B, note is smin and text (second syllable of "Clori") is missing.   M. 56, T, note 7 has printed ♯.   M. 58, B.c., note 3 has figure 4, a possible misprint for 6.   M. 123, B, text is "longamente".   M. 126, B.c., note 1, figure is 6; replaced by ♯ in edition.   M. 133, T, note 1 has printed cautionary ♯ (indicating ♮).   M. 137, B.c., note 3, figure is 6; replaced by ♯ in edition.   M. 141, B.c., figures ♯, 4, and 5 appear over note 1; given the tenor part in m. 142, the figures 4 and 5 would work better in that measure.

15. Per torbido mare

The vocal sections move generally in groups of six minims or two dotted semibreves, with the exception of a single nine-minim group (mm. 8, 23, 40, and 55 in this edition) near the end of each verse. The continuo part for the ritornello, labeled "a bene pl[a]cito", however, moves in groups of four dotted minims (see m. 26 and following) and cadences on what would be the second dotted minim of the final measure (m. 33). Performers must consider whether four dotted minims of the ritornello (if it is to be played at all) equal six minims in the vocal section, or if each dotted minim should be played in the time of a dotted semibreve. The ritornello was perhaps taken from another work and the composer failed to change the dotted minims to dotted semibreves.

M. 4, C (alto), note 4 has printed cautionary ♭.   M. 4, T, note 4 is e′; changed by printer to f′.   M. 17, B, note 5, text is "sèn".   M. 36, C, note 4 has printed cautionary ♭.   Mm. 54–55, T, beginning with last note of m. 54 and all notes of m. 55, text is "son placidi placidi ven", this last syllable under last three notes of m. 55; the second syllable of "venti" is missing; performers of the tenor part may wish to substitute "Per l'onda d'amore Son" on the last note of m. 54 and the first six notes of m. 55.   M. 56, C, two notes are sbr–sbr; T and B.c. have two tied notes, sbr–sbr; B has sbr–min.

16. Io, che piansi

Mm. 15–16, C, text is "pianto arsi al tuo ardor", with note 4 of m. 16 set to the syllable "-dor" in the source, but the rhyme scheme and line length of the sonnet would require the first line to end with "ardore" rather than "ardor"; also, the concatenation of [ar]-si͜_al tuo͜_ar-[dor] on notes 2 and 3 is awkward, so performers may wish to emend measures 15–16 in the following manner:

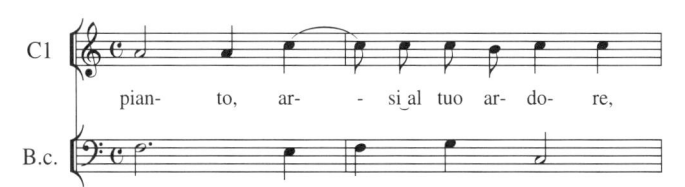

M. 34, B.c. has *A5*, indicating that the violins are to play in this section.   M. 76, B.c. has the cue "Tenor" for the canto primo solo, while at the beginning of the first solo (m. 13 in this edition) the cue is "Canto solo"; this reflects the alternative voice parts involving tenors referred to in the partbooks.   Mm. 90 and 94, B, notes 2–3, text is "amor".   M. 100, B, note 5 has ♯.   M. 116, T (canto secondo), note 4 has printed ♯.

17. Una fanciulla

C, T, and B, "Ritornello Tacet" appears before the first verse, though there is no indication in the B.c. partbook that the ritornello is to be played before the first verse. Below the music in that partbook appears the instruction "Si replica le prime due righe [sic] sino al finale con il suo ritornello à bene placito."; there are actually three staves that are repeated.

M. 6, T and B, text is "rubuto".   Mm. 10 and 34, B.c., figure ♯ appears to the left of the note; continuo players may wish to delay it and play a 4–3 suspension.   Mm. 40 and 42, T, text is "m'ha rubato il sen".   M. 49, B.c. has "finale tutti violini."   M. 50, T, notes 1–2 are cr–cr.   M. 51, B, notes 1–2 are dotted cr–scr.   M. 52, T, notes 2–3 are cr–cr.   M. 53, T, notes 3–4 are cr–cr.

18. Addio begl'occhi

M. 20, T, note 4 has printed ♯.   M. 49, B, note 3 has printed cautionary ♯ (indicating ♮).   Mm. 58–59, B.c., "Tenori" printed over the staff.   M. 60, B, meter (proportional) signature is **3**; B.c., meter (proportional) signature is $\frac{3}{1}$.   M. 67, B.c., note 1 has printed cautionary ♯ (indicating ♮).   Mm. 94–95, C, last note of m. 94 and two notes of m. 95, text is "morire".

Notes

1. Emil Bohn, *Bibliographie der Musik-Druckwerke bis 1700, welche in der Stadtbibliothek, der Bibliothek des Academischen Instituts für Kirchenmusik und der Königlichen und Universitäts-Bibliothek zu Breslau aufbewahrt werden* (1883; reprint, Hildesheim: Georg Olms Verlag, 1969), 273.

2. Errors and omissions may have been noted immediately following the print run at Vincenti's shop; small pieces of paper containing printed text corrections were pasted into the alto and tenor parts of "Or so come da sè," and the bass part of "Già brutto non son io" and "Spars'ho in pianto."

3. Except for the continuo part there is very little barring in the source.

4. Bohn, *Bibliographie der Musik-Druckwerke bis 1700*, v, and Brian Brooks, "Étienne Nau, Breslau 114 and the Early 17th-century Solo Violin Fantasia," *Early Music* 32 (2004): 49–72.

Recent Researches in the Music of the Baroque Era
Steven Saunders, general editor

Vol.	Composer: Title
1	Marc-Antoine Charpentier: *Judicium Salomonis*
2	Georg Philipp Telemann: *Forty-eight Chorale Preludes*
3	Johann Caspar Kerll: *Missa Superba*
4–5	Jean-Marie Leclair: *Sonatas for Violin and Basso continuo, Opus 5*
6	*Ten Eighteenth-Century Voluntaries*
7–8	William Boyce: *Two Anthems for the Georgian Court*
9	Giulio Caccini: *Le nuove musiche*
10–11	Jean-Marie Leclair: *Sonatas for Violin and Basso continuo, Opus 9 and Opus 15*
12	Johann Ernst Eberlin: *Te Deum; Dixit Dominus; Magnificat*
13	Gregor Aichinger: *Cantiones Ecclesiasticae*
14–15	Giovanni Legrenzi: *Cantatas and Canzonets for Solo Voice*
16	Giovanni Francesco Anerio and Francesco Soriano: *Two Settings of Palestrina's "Missa Papae Marcelli"*
17	Giovanni Paolo Colonna: *Messe a nove voci concertata con stromenti*
18	Michel Corrette: *"Premier livre d'orgue" and "Nouveau livre de noëls"*
19	Maurice Greene: *Voluntaries and Suites for Organ and Harpsichord*
20	Giovanni Antonio Piani: *Sonatas for Violin Solo and Violoncello with Cembalo*
21–22	Marin Marais: *Six Suites for Viol and Thoroughbass*
23–24	Dario Castello: *Selected Ensemble Sonatas*
25	*A Neapolitan Festa a Ballo and Selected Instrumental Ensemble Pieces*
26	Antonio Vivaldi: *The Manchester Violin Sonatas*
27	Louis-Nicolas Clérambault: *Two Cantatas for Soprano and Chamber Ensemble*
28	Giulio Caccini: *Nuove musiche e nuova maniera di scriverle (1614)*
29–30	Michel Pignolet de Montéclair: *Cantatas for One and Two Voices*
31	Tomaso Albinoni: *Twelve Cantatas, Opus 4*
32–33	Antonio Vivaldi: *Cantatas for Solo Voice*
34	Johann Kuhnau: *Magnificat*
35	Johann Stadlmayr: *Selected Magnificats*
36–37	Jacopo Peri: *Euridice: An Opera in One Act, Five Scenes*
38	Francesco Severi: *Salmi passaggiati (1615)*
39	George Frideric Handel: *Six Concertos for the Harpsichord or Organ (Walsh's Transcriptions, 1738)*
40	*The Brasov Tablature (Brasov Music Manuscript 808): German Keyboard Studies 1608–1684*
41	John Coprario: *Twelve Fantasias for Two Bass Viols and Organ and Eleven Pieces for Three Lyra Viols*

42	Antonio Cesti: *Il pomo d'oro (Music for Acts III and V from Modena, Biblioteca Estense, Ms. Mus. E. 120)*
43	Tomaso Albinoni: *Pimpinone: Intermezzi comici musicali*
44–45	Antonio Lotti: *Duetti, terzetti, e madrigali a piu voci*
46	Matthias Weckmann: *Four Sacred Concertos*
47	Jean Gilles: *Requiem (Messe des morts)*
48	Marc-Antoine Charpentier: *Vocal Chamber Music*
49	*Spanish Art Song in the Seventeenth Century*
50	Jacopo Peri: *"Le varie musiche" and Other Songs*
51–52	Tomaso Albinoni: *Sonatas and Suites, Opus 8, for Two Violins, Violoncello, and Basso continuo*
53	Agostino Steffani: *Twelve Chamber Duets*
54–55	Gregor Aichinger: *The Vocal Concertos*
56	Giovanni Battista Draghi: *Harpsichord Music*
57	*Concerted Sacred Music of the Bologna School*
58	Jean-Marie Leclair: *Sonatas for Violin and Basso continuo, Opus 2*
59	Isabella Leonarda: *Selected Compositions*
60–61	Johann Schelle: *Six Chorale Cantatas*
62	Denis Gaultier: *La Rhétorique des Dieux*
63	Marc-Antoine Charpentier: *Music for Molière's Comedies*
64–65	Georg Philipp Telemann: *Don Quichotte auf der Hochzeit des Comacho: Comic Opera-Serenata in One Act*
66	Henry Butler: *Collected Works*
67–68	John Jenkins: *The Lyra Viol Consorts*
69	*Keyboard Transcriptions from the Bach Circle*
70	Melchior Franck: *Geistliche Gesäng und Melodeyen*
71	Georg Philipp Telemann: *Douze solos, à violon ou traversière*
72	Marc-Antoine Charpentier: *Nine Settings of the "Litanies de la Vierge"*
73	*The Motets of Jacob Praetorius II*
74	Giovanni Porta: *Selected Sacred Music from the Ospedale della Pietà*
75	*Fourteen Motets from the Court of Ferdinand II of Hapsburg*
76	Jean-Marie Leclair: *Sonatas for Violin and Basso continuo, Opus 1*
77	Antonio Bononcini: *Complete Sonatas for Violoncello and Basso continuo*
78	Christoph Graupner: *Concerti Grossi for Two Violins*
79	Paolo Quagliati: *Il primo libro de' madrigali a quattro voci*
80	Melchior Franck: *Dulces Mundani Exilij Deliciae*
81	*Late-Seventeenth-Century English Keyboard Music*
82	*Solo Compositions for Violin and Viola da gamba with Basso continuo*
83	Barbara Strozzi: *Cantate, ariete a una, due e tre voci, Opus 3*
84	Charles-Hubert Gervais: *Super flumina Babilonis*

85	Henry Aldrich: *Selected Anthems and Motet Recompositions*
86	Lodovico Grossi da Viadana: *Salmi a quattro cori*
87	Chiara Margarita Cozzolani: *Motets*
88	Elisabeth-Claude Jacquet de La Guerre: *Cephale et Procris*
89	Sébastien Le Camus: *Airs à deux et trois parties*
90	Thomas Ford: *Lyra Viol Duets*
91	*Dedication Service for St. Gertrude's Chapel, Hamburg, 1607*
92	Johann Klemm: *Partitura seu Tabulatura italica*
93	Giovanni Battista Somis: *Sonatas for Violin and Basso continuo, Opus 3*
94	John Weldon: *The Judgment of Paris*
95–96	Juan Bautista Comes: *Masses. Parts 1–2*
97	Sebastian Knüpfer: *Lustige Madrigalien und Canzonetten*
98	Stefano Landi: *La morte d'Orfeo*
99	Giovanni Battista Fontana: *Sonatas for One, Two, and Three Parts with Basso continuo*
100	Georg Philipp Telemann: *Twelve Trios*
101	Fortunato Chelleri: *Keyboard Music*
102	Johann David Heinichen: *La gara degli Dei*
103	Johann David Heinichen: *Diana su l'Elba*
104	Alessandro Scarlatti: *Venere, Amore e Ragione*
105	*Songs with Theorbo (ca. 1650–1663)*
106	Melchior Franck: *Paradisus Musicus*
107	Heinrich Ignaz Franz von Biber: *Missa Christi resurgentis*
108	Johann Ludwig Bach: *Motets*
109–10	Giovanni Rovetta: *Messa, e salmi concertati, op. 4 (1639). Parts 1–2*
111	Johann Joachim Quantz: *Seven Trio Sonatas*
112	Petits motets *from the Royal Convent School at Saint Cyr*
113	Isabella Leonarda: *Twelve Sonatas, Opus 16*
114	Rudolph di Lasso: *Virginalia Eucharistica (1615)*
115	Giuseppe Torelli: *Concerti musicali, Opus 6*
116–17	Nicola Francesco Haym: *Complete Sonatas. Parts 1–2*
118	Benedetto Marcello: *Il pianto e il riso delle quattro stagioni*
119	Loreto Vittori: *La Galatea*
120–23	William Lawes: *Collected Vocal Music. Parts 1–4*
124	Marco da Gagliano: *Madrigals. Part 1*
125	Johann Schop: *Erster Theil newer Paduanen*
126	Giovanni Felice Sances: *Motetti a una, due, tre, e quattro voci (1638)*
127	Thomas Elsbeth: *Sontägliche Evangelien*
128–30	Giovanni Antonio Rigatti: *Messa e salmi, parte concertati. Parts 1–3*
131	*Seventeenth-Century Lutheran Church Music with Trombones*

132	Francesco Cavalli: *La Doriclea*
133	*Music for "Macbeth"*
134	Domenico Allegri: *Music for an Academic Defense (Rome, 1617)*
135	Jean Gilles: *Diligam te, Domine*
136	Silvius Leopold Weiss: *Lute Concerti*
137	*Masses by Alessandro Scarlatti and Francesco Gasparini*
138	Giovanni Ghizzolo: *Madrigali et arie per sonare et cantare*
139	Michel Lambert: *Airs from "Airs de différents autheurs"*
140	William Babell: *Twelve Solos for a Violin or Oboe with Basso Continuo. Book 1*
141	Giovanni Francesco Anerio: *Selva armonica (Rome, 1617)*
142–43	Bellerofonte Castaldi: *Capricci (1622). Parts 1–2*
144	Georg von Bertouch: *Sonatas a 3*
145	Marco da Gagliano: *Madrigals. Part 2*
146	Giovanni Rovetta: *Masses*
147	Giacomo Antonio Perti: *Five-Voice Motets for the Assumption of the Virgin Mary*
148	Giovanni Felice Sances: *Motetti a 2, 3, 4, e cinque voci (1642)*
149	*La grand-mére amoureuse, parodie d'Atys*
150	Andreas Hammerschmidt: *Geistlicher Dialogen Ander Theil*
151	Georg von Bertouch: *Three Sacred Cantatas*
152	Giovanni Maria Ruggieri: *Two Settings of the Gloria*
153	Alessandro Scarlatti: *Concerti sacri, opera seconda*
154	Johann Sigismund Kusser: *Adonis*
155	John Blow: *Selected Verse Anthems*
156	Anton Holzner: *Viretum pierium (1621)*
157	Alessandro Scarlatti: *Venere, Adone, et Amore*
158	Marc-Antoine Charpentier: *In nativitatem Domini canticum, H. 416*
159	Francesco Scarlatti: *Six Concerti Grossi*
160	Charles Avison: *Concerto Grosso Arrangements of Geminiani's Opus 1 Violin Sonatas*
161	Johann David Heinichen: *Selected Music for Vespers*
162–63	Francesco Gasparini: *Cantatas with Violins. Parts 1–2*
164–65	Antoine Boesset: *Sacred Music. Parts 1–2*
166	Andreas Hammerschmidt: *Selections from the "Gespräche" (1655–56) with Capellen*
167	Santiago de Murcia: *Cifras selectas de guitarra*
168	Gottfried Heinrich Stölzel: *German Te Deum*
169	Biagio Marini: *Compositioni varie per musica di camera, Opus 13*

CHECK FOR 3 PARTS